THE JOURNEY AHEAD

A New Roadmap to Collaboration in Your Firm

SANDRA WILEY

ISBN: 1489528768
ISBN 13: 9781489528766

Table of Contents

Foreword by L. Gary Boomer

The accounting profession is at a crossroads: a crossroads that suggests your biggest successes might also be your biggest challenges. This crossroads is exploring next generation client service. This crossroads is taking your employees and developing them into a community of individuals that work together for the greater good of the company. This crossroads is taking your firm leaders and molding them into advocates for change. If you ignore this crossroads, this forward progress of collaboration, you and your firm are likely to get left behind.

Stop and actively think about your clients. What are their needs? What are their expectations? Are they satisfied? What type of relationship do you have with them? Now stop and think about how you are working with them. Where do you want to take them? What are you doing to ensure that you aren't just doing a better job of what you have always done? With the changing mind-set of today's clients and the challenges the profession will face, a collaborative strategy for the future of your firm could very well be the difference between good enough and great.

The topic of collaboration has been swirling around the profession for years, but the rewards system was primarily for rugged individuals who could leverage resources. **Finally there is clear plan and path for truly changing your firm from a group of individuals sharing**

overhead to a team of collaborators creating something larger than any individual. These collaborators are able to support each other, be more productive, remain motivated, and ultimately create a firm that will thrive today and into the future. Sandra's practical approach in the pages ahead will set your firm on the road to developing three distinct collaborative pillars of success: (1) with your internal team, (2) with peers, and (3) with clients and business partners.

Collaboration is accelerated with technology, but technology alone will not create the attitude and environment required. Change is not only a possibility, but it's necessary to ensure a bright future for you and your firm. Change the culture and you *will* change results: grow revenue, attract and retain quality people, and improve profitability. Sandra gives you the keys to needed and valuable change in your firm's culture. As I look into the future with global implications and a competitive talent pool, I understand that firms must embrace new strategies today to ensure excellence in the future. This book gives you the knowledge and tools needed to succeed.

Innovation is based upon hindsight, foresight, and insight. As a thought leader in the accounting profession for over twenty-five years, I have had the pleasure of meeting and working with the best and the brightest individuals in this profession as well as some of the world's leading entrepreneurs. What sets these people apart from others is their ability and focus on taking existing resources to a higher level of value. They know their unique abilities and appreciate others' unique abilities. I have built my career on a vision of how technology accelerates planning, people, and processes along with the ability to identify new concepts, strategies, and a vision for leaders to follow. This gift extends to recognizing great talent with the capability and attitude to grow beyond their current status and ability if exposed to the right environment and opportunity to grow.

Foreword by L. Gary Boomer

I was introduced to and subsequently hired Sandra Wiley in 1995 when I was in the beginning stages of growing the Boomer Consulting team. She arrived with a background in banking and human resources. She began her career at Boomer Consulting as my assistant, but from the very beginning I knew she had the unique ability to communicate, motivate, and provide a vision for talent development that would change how firms manage their talent, how leaders would lead, and ultimately how the overall firm would change and evolve to a higher level of being. Today Sandra is one of our profession's top consultants and speakers with vast experience in leading firms.

As you read through Sandra's newest book, think about your clients, your firm, and the need for collaboration. Then ask yourself: Is your firm ready to collaborate? Is it prepared for change? If the answers are yes, follow through, and Sandra will show you the way!

L. Gary Boomer
CEO and Founder
Boomer Consulting, Inc.

Acknowledgments

To all of those who encouraged me, assisted me, believed in me, and ultimately allowed me the great honor of being a part of your life, thank you for the opportunity to write this labor of love for the profession.

To *Gary*, my mentor, my partner, and my friend: Thank you for your gift of seeing who I could be before I saw it in myself.

To my *amazing clients*: Thank you for allowing me the opportunity to learn from each of you every time we work together.

To *John*, the purveyor of fine words: Thank you for taking the musical notes that were my stories, my knowledge, and my words and turning them into a song.

To *Arianna, Jon, and Erin*, the final touch magicians: Thank you for your eagle eyes and your commitment to excellence.

To the entire collaborative *team at Boomer Consulting*: Thank you for inspiring me through your diligence to true collaboration every day, in every project.

To *Shannon*, my coach, my guide, and my teacher: Thank you for seeing my vision and encouraging me long before I ever began to write.

The Journey Ahead

To my *mom,* the person who has been with me every step of the way: Thank you for encouraging me my entire life to be the best I can be, to celebrate the good times, and not dwell too long on the tough times.

To *Charlie, Deanna, and Sarah*, the ones who hold my heart in their hands: Thank you for the memories you made for me as you grew and the amazing adults you have become.

To *Doug*, the love of my life: Thank you for always standing solidly beside me and walking with me on life's sometimes wild and crazy journey. The best is yet to come!

Introduction

Welcome to Your Future:

Prepare yourself for a journey that starts with the first chapter of this book and will never really end. Collaboration will become a foundational value of your firm; the only real question is whether that will be now or later. The pages ahead are the jump start plan for your leadership team to follow, like the GPS system that will help to guide you. It is not meant to be a "read me and reference me" book. It is truly a guide with tools and stories that will inspire and direct you. Therefore, I would suggest that you follow the steps below to ensure you get the true value that is afforded you:

1) **Form a Collaboration Task Force:** At the end of each chapter, you will find a worksheet or a tool that will help you take action for your firm in the topic addressed. These tools will be most valuable if you indeed work as a team to complete them. Choose the team carefully, and consider a blend of talents, age, education, and, most important, passion for ensuring the success of the firm.

2) **Work Through a Chapter at a Time:** Encourage your task force to read a chapter, meet regularly, discuss the topic, and then act on the tool that is available. Most important, I don't believe in rushing through the process. Some topics and tools you will fly through;

others will need to be digested and discussed in more depth. It will depend on where your firm is in their development.

3) **Talk About the End Game:** As you take your steps in the journey, stop occasionally and refocus your vision. There are times when firm leadership gets stuck on a vision for the firm that does not work anymore. New information, skills, technology, information, experience, and pure wisdom will make the old vision go out of focus, and we will need to sharpen the new view. The Collaboration Task Force may blur the old vision of the firm and will then help to focus in on a new, crystal-clear vision for the future.

4) **Keep Everyone in the Loop:** This book and the wisdom and stories that are stored in the pages are not meant to be hidden in a back room committee. The move from a silo-based firm to a collaborative work force is exciting and should be shared with the entire firm. Ensure that the task force is seeking information from others as well as sharing progress on a regular basis. Communication is essential to the success of the process.

The book is titled *The Journey Ahead* for a reason. A journey inspires many emotions, including excitement, frustration, fear, and exhilaration. Your team may well feel one or all of these emotions as you forge ahead and build a truly collaborative culture, but the true joy and reward come in *making* the journey and seeing the exciting changes along the way.

Make the commitment, build the team, communicate the progress, and watch the magic happen!

—Sandra

Chapter One: Why Collaborate?

Tom Mitchum was still upset as he walked into the paneled conference room at Mitchum, Jones & Templeton and sank into one of the leather chairs. Both Sam Jones and Bill Templeton were already there in response to Tom's hastily called meeting.

"I have bad news," Tom said. "I just got off the phone with Art Majeski at Monolith Industries. They are leaving us to go with Taylor & Brooks!"

"You're kidding, aren't you?" Sam Jones asked. "They've been with us for nearly a decade. How could this happen? What reasons did he give?"

"You know Art; he's always played it close to the vest," Tom said. "But he did let on that T&B did exceptional work on a piece of business at one of Monolith's divisions, and I guess they were able to leverage that into a shot at the entire account."

"This is terrible!" said Bill Templeton. "Losing their billings will cost us plenty. And they're the third client we've lost to Taylor this year. What do those guys do that we don't? I mean, I thought we were in solid with Monolith."

"Art did tell me that they put together a contract at a fixed fee for the project and brought it in on time and on budget," Tom added. "He called

1

it a value agreement. *Apparently they no longer bill clients by the hour at T&B."*

Sam Jones spoke up. "I can see how that would be attractive to Monolith," he said. *"But how can T&B do that? We've always tracked our time and billed for it. Sometimes we have to take write-downs, of course, but that's just the way we've always done things around here."*

"There may be more to this story," replied Tom. "Art told me that T&B virtually camped out at their place—worked side by side with their staff in a collaborative way—and came up with a handful of ideas on how they could run their business more efficiently. Without being asked, they reviewed last year's tax returns and spotted a huge opportunity for Monolith in doing cost segregation."

"Well, it's not like we've been asleep at the switch," countered Bill Templeton. "But I'm not comfortable doing things like that gratis."

"You are right about one thing, Bill," said the managing partner. "We can't let this go on. We have to figure this out. I'm going to see if I can find out more about how T&B operates. And I want you two to touch base with every major account to see where we stand with them."

■

If the fictional scenario above seems farfetched, you'd be mistaken. The economic downturn has led to increased competition among CPA firms, of course, but the changes go deeper than that. We are in a results-based economy now, not an effort-oriented one. And, as we move through a service-based economy to a digital one, the need for new thinking about how work gets done will change with it.

Firms that simply try to do a better job of what they've always done are likely to be left behind. You'd be hard-pressed to find a CPA firm that doesn't say they deliver good service and view their relationship with clients as a positive one. Yet the hard reality may be quite different, viewed from the client's point of view.

In a recent survey of CPA firm clients sponsored by CCH, the accounting and tax software giant, 36 percent of business clients—one in three—said they would switch firms and gave the primary reason as failure on the part of their current firm to keep pace with their changing needs. Some 55 percent said they were being actively prospected by other CPA firms.

Collaboration makes the difference and bridges the gap between internal team members, peer firms, and the vendors we work with so closely. Collaboration is the act of working with another person to complete a task with the end result being stronger due to collective thinking. In relation to your team, collaboration enables ideas and tasks to be shared by the group and eliminates silos that have existed in the past. Collaboration with your clients will keep you involved on a more frequent basis and will make relationships stronger by engaging with them as their needs change. Finally, engaging with your vendors allows for gathering and using outside expertise to join with internal resources and collaboratively build processes and systems that will make the overall firm stronger.

Consider the following research points.

Client Needs Are Growing

Forty-five percent of business clients and 24 percent of individual clients say support needs will increase in the next year, while just 5 percent of business clients and 7 percent of individual clients say needs would decrease. The potential for new opportunities to bring value to your clients exists, but only if firm leadership finds new ways to encourage relationship building with current clients. The potential to provide increased value with current clients can happen with the appropriate communication and discipline to build out new services.

Increased Need for Specialized Services

Fifty-five percent of business and 29 percent of individual clients report the number of specialized services they need from their CPA firm is growing. If firms continue to do what they have always done, they are sure to fail in the future. Clients expect new services that will meet their changing business models, and they look to their firm professionals to come to them with new ideas.

Increase Client Satisfaction

While 79 percent of business clients say they are *generally* satisfied with their CPA firm, of that group, only 17 percent are *completely* satisfied. Understanding how satisfied your clients are with your firm and then implementing strategies to improve has long been a staple in ensuring that exceptional client service is being exhibited in professional services firms. A client service survey is essential in the process.

Provide a Seat at the Table

The top reason clients would consider leaving their firm is that the firm does not regularly check with them on their changing needs. The firms that are not in touch with their clients are those that lose a client, and the firm leaders look at each other and say, "I had no idea they were unhappy." The hard reality is that they did not know because they were out of touch with their clients. Great firms are those that consistently meet with their clients and also ensure that many individuals in the firm have a relationship with the client, not just one person.

Showcase Expertise

Firms' overall expertise is a top driver in firm selection for business clients. For individuals, referrals most often drive selection. In a collaborative work environment, hiring and retaining team members at all levels with various experience and expertise is imperative to showcasing a firm of value.

Expectations Are Changing

Research published in the *Harvard Business Review* says the most important thing customers want is to reduce their effort in doing business. In the CCH survey mentioned earlier, business clients identified "efficient and quick service" as one of the three most important things they want from their CPA firm.

Consumer-based service experiences are driving your clients' service expectations like never before. In banking, for example, people routinely use cloud computing and mobile phones to conduct business. They have no patience with standing in line or adhering to "bankers' hours." Similarly, people go online to make airline reservations and have their boarding passes delivered directly to their phone to eliminate paper and save time.

In addition, business clients are leveraging technology, and they expect their firms to do the same, whether it's working in the cloud or digitizing more of their environment. After all, today's new digital infrastructure has fundamentally changed the way most of us do business—and changed your clients' expectations as well. Today, clients expect you to be connected to them. They want you to be available to help them when they need it.

Collaboration addresses each of these issues by forging tighter bonds with clients—collaborating with them—to look for ways to add value beyond traditional compliance services. The key is to create value at every client "touch point," not just in the services you provide but in the way you deliver those services.

Visit www.boomer.com/collaboration and download

Collaboration Tool #1

Is Your Firm Ready to Collaborate?

Chapter Two: What Does True Collaboration Look Like?

Tom Mitchum leaned against the doorjamb in Bill Templeton's office. Stacks of file folders seemed to fill most of the available space, elbowing aside pictures of Bill's family and a crystal plaque from the Rotary Club. "What have you learned from visiting with Ajax and your other key clients?" Tom asked.

"Those guys at Taylor & Brooks are after Ajax, too!" Templeton said. "They were introduced through a relationship banker at First Trust, according to Steve Meyer, the CFO. Good thing I'm tight with Steve, because he told me a lot about their operation."

"What did you find out?" Mitchum asked. "Tell me and I'll fill you in on what I've learned as well."

"It turns out that T&B has moved the whole organization toward 'value pricing,' on both the accounting and tax sides," Bill explained. "They sit with clients and map out a year's worth of work, then get a signed contract for a fee everyone agrees to."

"Whoa! How do they make sure they are making a profit?"

"According to Steve they have enough experience to know how much time things should take and use that as a basis for quoting the work,"

Bill said. "I suppose some jobs come in under budget and some don't. Or maybe they use 'change orders' like our friends in construction."

"Was there anything else?" Bill asked.

"Steve said they made a big deal about how they collaborate with their clients," Bill replied. "Each partner is obligated to spend fifty hours per year 'off the clock,' meeting with their key clients. He said that encourages people to open up and share their problems. I bet that's how they landed the cost segregation work at Monolith that we talked about at the last meeting."

"No doubt about it." Tom nodded. "Monolith told me they didn't charge anything for analyzing last year's tax returns. But I found out some other interesting facts as well from a potential new hire who interviewed with them."

Bill leaned forward in his chair, anxious to hear what his managing partner had to say.

Tom said, "Apparently they no longer use time and billing software. She spoke with associates at T&B, and they rave about not having to track every minute of their time. It was a real morale boost, she said.

"There's something else, Bill. Apparently they put together cross-functional teams assigned to work on each business client. Even new people get assigned to teams like that, rather than starting out doing audit work or filling out tax returns."

Bill stiffened. "I don't know about that. After all, what can a junior person offer? Whatever happened to paying your dues in this business, like you and I did? My old accounting professor would roll over in his grave!"

"Well, I'm sure there are senior people on the teams," Tom replied. "But they all get client contact and come up with fresh ideas and help solve problems. It certainly was enough for the candidate to accept their offer instead of ours, even though the starting salary was lower."

■

In our networked world, nearly everyone is connected. Some eight hundred million "friends" are on Facebook at last count. And according to Google's Eric Schmidt, Chinese language web pages will dominate search returns in five years or so. Around twenty million people joined Google's new platform in 2011 over a few weeks. And by 2020, twelve *billion* mobile devices will connect to the Internet, according to recent industry forecasts.

But simply being connected is not enough—especially when the way forward runs smack dab into the traditional independent, competitive, "lone wolf" mind-set many of us grew up with. When everyone is connected, collaboration becomes the game changer—with a boost from the right technology. Collaboration adds power and helps the many do what no one person can accomplish alone.

Collaboration is really about people, though, not technologies. After all, if technology was the path to success, the firm with the best toys would win. Technology can tip the scales, but success really calls for having the right people saying "yes"—and then participating.

Types of Collaboration

"Coming together is a beginning, staying together is progress, and working together is success." —Henry Ford

This quote demonstrates how necessary it is that we collaborate with one another to find advances. The pack of wolves that hunts together is more likely to catch its prey than the lone wolf. Likewise, a team of scientists brings more to the table and is better able to solve problems than one scientist cloistered away in his or her ivory tower. Throughout natural history, collaboration has been a necessary part of life that leads toward realization of a desired outcome.

In today's competitive business environment, a firm that wants to innovate and succeed must be collaborative. In this "do more with less" reality, it takes ongoing teamwork to produce innovative, cost-effective, and targeted solutions for clients and the firms that serve them. Survival may depend on how well a firm can combine the potential of its people, the quality of the information they possess, and their ability (read: willingness) to share that knowledge.

But here's a common problem that needs to be overcome: the collaboration that is so critical is often blocked by knowledge-hoarding "silo" structures and the "silo mentality" that have traditionally led to internal power struggles, competition, lack of cooperation, and loss of productivity.

Conceptually it is useful to describe collaboration as the act of people working with people to get something done at work (or at play). In this instance we're talking about work, often with distributed participants. The collaboration practices are diverse, so it is helpful to see what general patterns are at play. In the next three sections, we will discuss the three most common patterns.

Team Collaboration

In **team collaboration**, the members of the group are known, and there are clear task interdependencies, expected reciprocity, and explicit timelines and goals. To achieve the goal, members must fulfill their tasks within the stated time. Team collaboration often suggests that while there is explicit leadership, the participants cooperate on an equal footing and will receive equal recognition. An example is a project aimed at mapping process bottlenecks in tax prep and finding ways to cure them. Team members get a deadline and a set of resources to work with.

Some groups in the workplace form through natural selection, as a result of similarity, proximity, and prior acquaintance. It's human nature to turn to these "collaboration regulars" for support, encouragement, or to share ideas. One example is a team of auditors working together on a list of clients. The potential for smooth interaction and strong commitment is high. There can be less hesitancy to speak up and disagree, which is a good thing and important to creative problem solving.

But researchers have uncovered a negative aspect of team collaboration that needs to be considered. It's called the "Common Knowledge Effect," a term coined by Daniel Gigone and Reid Hastie, and supported by Stanford, Northwestern, and Columbia research. They found that in groups where the majority of members possess the same knowledge, that knowledge becomes the basis of discussion. Minority-held information by individuals is clouded out of the decision-making process. There is a rush to consider the problem as solved or the right idea as established.

This is a problem for too-familiar collaboration groups. Valuable information can be missed or never even considered. This is not about challenging others' analysis and assumptions but just plain missing critical bits of information.

Community Collaboration

In **community collaboration**, there is a shared area of interest, but the goal centers on learning, rather than specific tasks. People share and build knowledge, rather than complete projects. Membership in the community may be limited and explicit or open to anyone. Similarly, participation is ongoing. Periods of participation are often open or "ongoing."

Membership is often on equal footing, but more experienced practitioners may have more status or power in the community. Reciprocity is within the group but not always one-to- one (*"I did this for you, now you do this for me"*).

An example within a firm would be using knowledge management software to avoid "reinventing the wheel" by sharing documents across the firm or posting answers to frequently asked audit or tax questions to cut down on interruptions and take the pressure off a clogged e-mail system. An obvious payoff is capturing the knowledge partners and seniors carry around in their heads so that it does not leave the firm when someone retires or leaves for "greener pastures."

One outside community example is The Boomer Technology Circles™, where firms from across the country come together to learn from each other and share their experiences in a nonthreatening way.

Boomer Consulting, Inc. has over fifteen years of experience in facilitating communities. Boomer Consulting, Inc. started with The Boomer Technology Circles™ and then expanded to The CIO Advantage™, The Producer Circle™, The CEO Advantage™, and The Talent Development Advantage™.

All of these communities provide participants with access to experts and the opportunity to develop peer relationships. In most communities we ask firms to send two or more participants who act as a team. This approach bridges gaps between different, unique abilities.

The CPAs and firms that get the most value from communities are those who contribute and provide confidence to their peers. Learning is a two-way street. You must be vulnerable to learn and willing to teach. The communities raise the level of success for all participants. Also having access to expertise outside of their firm provides great value, even for internal experts. The exchange among expert peers results in learning, increased confidence, and improved clarity.

Network Collaboration

Network collaboration steps beyond the relationship-centric nature of team and community collaboration. And this is where it gets interesting. Network collaboration starts with individual action and self-interest and accrues to the network. Both membership and timelines are open and unbounded. There are no explicit roles. Members most likely do not know all the other members. Power is distributed. This form of collaboration has been busted wide open with the advent of new online tools, a response to the overwhelming volume of information we are creating and the number of people we can connect with. The tools expose us to possibility, remind us of the overwhelming volume, and offer us ways to share the task of coping with that volume.

Examples of network collaboration range from open source software solutions like Linux, to Wikipedia, the free online encyclopedia that in fact drove Microsoft to abandon its Encarta project. Network collaboration can benefit a team, a community of practice, as well as the wider network of people or stakeholders interested in the topic. This sort of network activity benefits the individual and a network of people reciprocally over time. The reciprocity connection is remote and undefined. Those who contribute act in self-interest but provide a network-wide benefit.

Examples of Collaboration in the Workplace

BMW and Toyota——Competitive Collaboration

BMW and Toyota have announced they will collaborate in two areas: the companies will share costs and knowledge for electric car battery research, and BMW will supply diesel engines to Toyota. Toyota owns the luxury brand Lexus, and therefore BMW and Toyota directly compete in the luxury car segment. Both companies have a significant collaboration track record.

Toyota will reportedly use BMW's 1.6 and 2-liter diesel engines for cars sold in Europe beginning in 2014. This is reportedly the first time Toyota has procured an engine from a competitor. According to a story by Yoshio Takahashi and Kenneth Maxwell in the December 2, 2011, edition of the *Wall Street Journal*, the collaboration will reduce BMW's engine production costs per unit by increasing volume.

Value creation is at the heart of this collaboration. "We think that this collaboration will allow for development of next-generation batteries to be done faster and to a higher level," Toyota Executive Vice President Takeshi Uchiyamada said at a news conference. Both companies will share the costs of battery development.

Collaboration among competitors works best when the effort involves eliminating redundancy in nondifferentiating processes. Under-the-hood processes in an automobile are not part of a company's market or product perception. Two companies that each make hot sauce might use the same bottling equipment. Two newspapers in the same market might use the same printing presses. Entire industries participate in consortiums for purchasing, saving each competing company substantial money.

Cisco Systems—Internal Collaboration

An excellent example of collaboration comes from Cisco Systems. Here an internal effort to improve collaboration had dramatic payoffs. The organization has embraced what's known as Enterprise 2.0, which it defines as "a system of Web-based technologies that provide rapid and agile collaboration, information sharing, emergence and integration capabilities in the extended enterprise," according to CTO Padmasree Warrior, who shared these results from collaborative initiatives at a recent technology conference:

- **Cost savings:** $172 million in travel savings, $4 million in support cost saved using an internal "Wiki," and $82 million in real estate and related cost savings.

- **Employee productivity:** $277 million in employee time savings; $27 million per year in approver productivity.

- **Customer intimacy:** 45 percent increase in specialist interaction with customers, improved product design by including customers in the process, and 1,700 additional hours of customer interaction—without travel.

- **Competitive differentiation:** Acquisitions took eight days on average versus forty-five, resulting in $137 million in margin improvement through faster deal approval. In addition, collaborative leadership resulted in twenty-eight priorities per year versus one or two.

Corporations like BMW, Toyota, and Cisco have access to resources to collaborate on a large scale, but accounting firms have opportunities to take advantage as well.

Stambaugh Ness PC—Top-to-Bottom Collaboration

Over the years, a top-to-bottom emphasis on collaboration and continuous improvement has become part of the firm's DNA, according to Thomas Moul, CPA, partner, and chief financial officer at Stambaugh Ness PC, a two-office York, Pennsylvania, firm that's become the "go-to" firm in south central Pennsylvania and bordering Maryland.

Thomas Moul, CPA,
partner, and chief financial officer
Stambaugh Ness PC
www.stambaughness.com
York, Pennsylvania

As reported in CCH *Partners* magazine, Moul cited a round of small-group meetings at the nine-partner firm aimed at dissecting what worked and what didn't during the 2012 filing season. Admins, reviewers, and partners shared their ideas on ways to tweak the firm's processes. "We keep challenging the way we do things," Moul says, "and looking for ways to use technology more effectively."

Until the 2008 downturn, Stambaugh Ness enjoyed double-digit growth, year over year, in part because of a decision the partners made around 2003 to adopt a strengths-based culture that encourages and rewards teamwork.

Everyone in the firm participated in the Strength Builder program, aimed at identifying what each person was best at, and then capitalizing on those strengths. To drive the culture change more effectively, the firm moved away from a traditional approach to partner compensation so that those who played to their strengths would be rewarded for it.

"One of our partners seems to be best at business development, so that is his entire focus," Moul says. Two partners are strongest and well connected in the architecture, engineering, and construction (AEC) niche and focus their time and effort on those clients. Others zero in on nonprofit or governmental clients.

Another example is the firm's Business Triage Team, a group of CPAs assembled to deliver effective turnaround and restructuring services to companies in distress. The team is geared specifically to quickly analyze financial and business issues to provide insight and ideas on immediate challenges business owners face, typically involving cash flow, cost containment, and financing negotiations.

TYS LLP—A CPA Firm That's Different in Fundamental Ways

Glen Thomas, Chris York, and Tim Shortsleeve all felt there was a better way to conduct business, so they formed a new kind of accounting firm in 2010—one that is collaborative, innovative, and on the leading edge. TYS LLP, officed in San Ramon, California, and Rochester, New York, is different in fundamental ways, both internally and externally.

Glen Thomas, CPA, partner
TYS LLP
www.tysllp.com
San Ramon, California

Chris York, CPA, partner
TYS LLP
www.tysllp.com
San Ramon, California

Tim Shortsleeve, CPA,
CITP, partner
TYS LLP
www.tysllp.com
Rochester, New York

"We are in a profession that is two centuries old and steeped in two-hundred-year-old ways of doing things," says managing shareholder Glen Thomas. "We believe that for us to be successful and for the profession to be successful things have to change."

For example, firm management is handled using a collaborative model, rather than a traditional hierarchy. "All decisions are not necessarily made from the top down," Thomas says. For example, managers meet at year-end to recommend how to split up the nonowner bonus pool.

"We want to teach our management group how to make decisions so they will be prepared to be owners when it is appropriate for them to become owners."

The firm painstakingly created its own Collaborative Operating System, based on agreements that spell out how everyone agrees to communicate, Thomas says. "Not only how we speak but how we agree to listen." Everyone in the firm signs off on the Collaborative Operating System as well as agreements that cover Conflict Resolution and Accountability. "These agreements give us a framework for how we can collaborate effectively. We do everything we can to build a level of trust in our organization that allows people to speak more freely, openly, and honestly."

Another thing that sets TYS apart is its results-only operating environment, in which anyone can work whenever and wherever they want, so long as the work gets done. "We do not track time, so we do not bill clients based on the hours involved," Thomas says. "In the billable dollar environment, there is a constant focus on *us* internally, in terms of managing resources in the most efficient way for *us*, which is not necessarily providing our clients with the best possible service.

The payoff: in an economy where firms are happy to stay even or grow by 5 percent, TYS is at 20 percent growth for 2012, and profitability is twice what the firm budgeted. As Thomas put it, "That's because we set targets and hold people accountable. It's also because we share the results throughout the firm. One-third of the profits are shared by the nonowners."

Brigante, Cameron, Watters & Strong LLP— Using Technology as a Tool for Collaboration

Brigante, Cameron, Watters & Strong LLP, a four-partner firm in Torrance, California, is an early adopter of technology. Managing Partner John Cameron, CPA, who trained as an engineer prior to becoming a CPA, has a feel for technology and how it can help streamline processes. "We started back in 1999 before other firms were doing it," he says, in a recent article in CCH *First Choice* newsletter. "It caused a few bruises, but it was worth it because we can do more with fewer people."

John Cameron, CPA,
managing partner
Brigante, Cameron, Watters &
Strong LLP
www.bcws.com
Torrance, California

He had the firm begin using E-Pace, which later was purchased by CCH and morphed into ProSystem fx° Engagement. "It was the first program that allowed us to get financial information electronically from a client and produce a financial statement and tax return without a lot of manual labor," Cameron says. "Today's modern version of it, ProSystem fx Engagement, is about seventy percent faster than the old manual methods."

One thing the firm has clients do today is submit their information electronically in advance. "We can review their information and prepare a trial balance before we ever go out and do field work," Cameron says. "We can walk in the door with a financial statement and do the work much faster. It adds a lot of credibility when we can walk in the door and show them financial statements on an iPad," Cameron says.

Another payoff is that the firm's professionals can work with clients on strategic issues, generating additional business, and helping solidify their relationships with clients.

His advice for other firms? "Step back and take a look at what you have been doing and why you are doing it. If you just adapt technology to what you were doing, you are not saving time, improving workflow, or helping your clients," Cameron says. "Even now, when we are automated end-to-end, every year, we ask, 'Why are we doing it this way?' and look for ways to improve."

Armanino McKenna LLP—Firm-Wide Collaboration

One firm that seems to be doing nearly everything right is Armanino McKenna LLP, one of the twenty-five "Best of the Best" accounting firms in the nation. Managing partner Andy Armanino, CPA, can flip open his laptop and with a few keystrokes quickly see where the firm stands—that day—in terms of charge hours, realization, billing and collection, profitability by service line, and other key performance indicators (KPIs).

Andy Armanino, CPA,
managing partner
Armanino McKenna LLP
www.amllp.com
San Ramon, California

"Previously, those KPIs were difficult to get at, requiring a lot of heavy lifting by our IT team, he says. "We might do it in advance of a partner meeting, but the rest of the time we'd wonder about it. You might see people with their heads down and figure you're doing OK. But that's not the way we want to run our business."

The need for up-to-the-minute business intelligence is just as essential to the kind of growth-oriented middle market firms Armanino McKenna serves. "We want to be the go-to resource for the CFO group—on their speed dial—not just on finance issues but with business process or people issues that will help them grow their businesses," added Matt Armanino, Andy's brother and COO at the firm.

Matt Armanino, partner,
chief operating officer
Armanino McKenna LLP
www.amllp.com
San Ramon, California

That holistic approach underpins year after year of double-digit growth and development of a robust consulting practice that now contributes about one-third of the firm's annual revenue. "We don't want to be a product provider, selling audits or tax returns," he says. "We want to understand what the client needs, where they want to be in the future, and how to help them get there."

The firm's IT consulting practice had already been working with clients to show them how to use executive dashboards and business analytics to help run their businesses, respond quickly to market challenges, be more aggressive and make better decisions. "We realized we needed the same kind of information ourselves, so we decided to drink our own Kool-Aid," Matt says.

The firm kicked off a project internally to develop a custom business intelligence (BI) solution tailored to the firm's needs using a web-based platform called QlikView, a second-generation BI product that now rides on top of ProSystem fx® Practice Management and provides an easy-to-use graphical interface that partners of the firm can use to review firm-wide metrics or drill down to get specific performance data on individual clients, engagements, offices, or staff.

"One of our core values is continuous improvement, and this tool supports that effectively," Matt explains. For example, top-level numbers for the valuation practice might be on track, but drill down and you discover charge hours for two people are way off. You investigate and find one person on vacation and the other in need of guidance. "That might have been masked before because the high-level results looked OK," Matt says. "Now we can see areas where you can drive continuous improvement."

Andy picked up the story thread: "The tool we deployed gave us wonderful information. It allowed us to see where our business was heading, where we could make changes and take advantage of opportunities."

Working together, Armanino and CCH developed ProSystem *fx* Practice Intelligence, which consists of the QlikView platform and a custom version of Armanino's dashboard that accesses Practice Management data files. Armanino McKenna acts as the implementation and consulting partner, working with other CPA firms to tailor the solution to their specific needs.

"It's a solution that can be deployed in a matter of weeks, not months, and that users can learn in a few hours," Matt says. "It's an app-like experience. If you know how to use an iPhone or Google, you can use this product to answer the 'how are we doing' questions."

Armanino McKenna does a lot more to set itself apart from the competition. "To serve clients the way we do requires attracting the right people and making them feel empowered," says Andy Armanino. Two specific examples:

- **Staff and manager advisory boards.** Staff members from across the firm, elected by their peers, serve on an advisory board that meets monthly and is empowered to help the firm solve problems. "It gives our young stars a chance to get their feet wet in a leadership role," Andy said. A similar board, elected by the firm's manager group, meets monthly and plays a key role in driving initiatives.

- **A quarterly "investor call" with the staff.** Unlike many firms that prefer to keep financial matters close to the vest, Armanino McKenna holds webinars, updating everyone in the firm on key firm metrics, statistical information, goals, and key wins. "We've decided that kind of openness is a risk we are willing to take. We want our people to feel part of the place and engaged in moving the firm forward," Andy says.

Visit www.boomer.com/collaboration and download

Collaboration Tool #2

The Team Collaboration Survey

Chapter Three: Is Your Firm Culture in Need of Change?

The waiter cleared away Tom Mitchum's half-eaten lunch. "We need to get down to business," he said to his partners, Sam Jones and Bill Templeton. "I don't have much of an appetite today anyway," he muttered. "Let me begin while you two finish up."

Jones speared the last forkful of chicken salad, and Templeton nodded. "Go ahead," Sam said and grinned. "You could stand to lose a pound or two anyway." You could tell the three partners liked to rib each other.

Mitchum smiled, then turned serious. "I decided we should meet off-site, away from the phones and interruptions," he began. "We really have to make some changes in the way the firm is being run. You know we lost Monolith and a couple other smaller corporate accounts, and just last week one of our best tax managers left for Taylor & Brooks, too."

"Tracy was good people," Sam nodded. "I was sorry to see her go. She said something in her exit interview that really got to me, although I am not sure I believe it."

"What was that?" Mitchum asked. "We can't afford to lose any more good people. It's hard enough to recruit top talent these days."

Jones leaned forward so as not to be overheard. "Apparently we talk about valuing work/life balance and letting people work from home, but when they ask to do it, there are repercussions."

Bill Templeton spoke up then. "Dammit. We were in the heat of tax season, and she was always wanting to be at home with her kids. As a manager she needed to be here on site to review returns and keep the work flowing. We have to get the work out, no matter what!"

"There's no need to get defensive, Bill," Tom said. "What does T&B offer that we don't?"

"Apparently they set staff people up with mirror-image systems at home so that they can be there for the family," Jones explained. "In fact their setup allows for remote access from anywhere, even Starbucks for all I know."

"Well, the idea of remote access scares the bejeezus out of me," Templeton said. "What about the security of client data? And more to the point, how do you know people are really working and not watching videos or chatting on FaceTube or whatever."

"I think you mean Facebook and YouTube," Tom said with a grin. "It feels to me like the real issue here is a lack of trust and some kind of disconnect between what we are saying and what is really happening. Did Tracy share anything else during her exit interview?"

Sam thought for a moment. "I don't have my notes in front of me, but I recall that she said the firm culture has changed since she started working for us. There's competition for attention and not enough sharing of information. She said we were 'siloed.'"

"Did she give an example?" Tom asked.

"There were several times when people on the audit staff would come to her with tax questions because we were too busy and—how did she put it—not approachable. She didn't know how to account for that time because it was an audit client, not a tax client."

"Listen, you guys, we need to get on top of this," Tom said. "We can't afford to lose any more good people. They are too hard to find in today's economy." The managing partner looked to Sam. "You've been handling HR issues for us. What do you think we should do now?

"I have been reading about conducting 'stay interviews' with the key people in your firm to find out what they like and dislike and how to improve," Sam said. "I think we should make a list and start doing that. We need to know where we stand."

"That's for sure," Tom said, nodding in agreement. "But we need to be willing to make changes based on what we find out, or things will get even worse. Let's get started with that."

■

Understanding Your Firm's Culture

Trying to define corporate culture sometimes feels like pressing your thumb down on a watermelon seed—it will slip away from you. It is intangible—a state of mind, a feeling, a collective consciousness embedded within a firm and its employees. If you ask twenty managing partners to define corporate culture, you will get twenty different responses.

Today we realize that culture can be defined and it can be changed. Too many firms discount the value of a coherent company culture, or they have limited knowledge about how to develop it. They take command of business disciplines that connect to profit margins and neglect the firm's emotional health; but, in fact, the two complement one another.

Think about your own culture. Does it ebb and flow with the economy? How might your employees describe your changing culture? Would they say that you were fun, relaxed, and open to new ideas a few years ago? (Remember when we were all struggling to find staff and were literally giving massages and big bonuses to everyone just to keep the average person happy?)

Those same individuals might say that now they feel a very different culture exists. Today, the massages are gone, and the bonuses have dried up. Employees are being told they are part of the best quality staff ever, yet they are getting less and expected to do more. The culture that was portrayed five years ago could not be sustained for the long term.

When considering your firm's culture, especially if it needs to change in response to such factors as competition, loss of valued staff to other firms, or the need to accommodate various generational or gender-based differences, it helps to take some time to understand the basics of corporate culture. Fortunately, there is a growing body of knowledge on the subject.

Four Categories of Corporate Culture

Dave Hofferberth and Jeanne Urich of SPI Research categorized corporate culture broadly in four different categories, as part of a 2012 survey of professional service organizations. See which one best describes your firm:

1. *Creative.* In creative cultures, the primary driver is self-expression. Leaders celebrate individuals and teams who break the mold with new innovations. A fluid organization structure typically contains self-organizing work teams and collaborative project groups. Creative cultures foster an environment where radical course change is possible. One example is Apple's switch from PCs to the wildly successful iPod and iPad. The environment can be cult-like, especially when there's a dynamic or visionary leader who can inspire the team to drink the Kool-Aid regardless of the consequences.

2. *Collaborative.* In collaborative cultures, the main drivers are teamwork and building consensus. Leaders often base decision making on a shared view of the desired results. The downside of collaborative cultures can be slow decision making and too much time spent on evaluating alternatives. Leaders value trustworthiness and teamwork above creativity and aggressiveness. Collaborative companies tend to develop deep, long-lasting relationships with clients and typically use customer satisfaction as a performance metric. Collaborative companies (think H-P under Dave Packard) use matrix management and complex reporting structures.

3. *Competitive.* In competitive cultures, personal or team achievement drives the bus. "Winning" is the way everyone keeps score, and the focus is on beating the competition. You will see quarterly competitive hit lists that aim to squash the competitive enemy of the month. They value personal knowledge and killer instincts, celebrating individual achievement more than teamwork. Leaders love management dashboards that reveal trends and market-share gains. Overly competitive structures may blur the line between competing and cheating.

4. Controlled. In controlled cultures, the primary driver is order and alignment based on clear goals and objectives. Leaders create hierarchical reporting structures where power and authority are vested at the top. They value quarterly improvement metrics and benchmarks to determine operational excellence. The organization highly values annual and quarterly business plans and key performance measurements. Overly controlled cultures can lead to excessive bureaucracy, red tape, and rules. Employees may feel unable to make decisions without management review and approval. In out-of-balance controlled cultures, you may find a caste system where individual competency and achievement take a backseat in favor of maintaining order and the status quo.

Interestingly, the 2012 PS Maturity Model™ asked 216 professional service organizations to identify their culture. Some 60 percent ticked the "collaborative" box, while 20 percent saw themselves as "creative." Only 10 percent admitted to being "competitive," and the remaining 10 percent said they were "controlled."

One wonders how truly collaborative the responding professional firms actually are. Some of those responses may amount to wishful thinking. All too often efforts to collaborate are sabotaged by political games and turf battles higher up in an organization. Consider, for example, that Microsoft developed a viable tablet computer more than a decade ago but failed to bring it to the market and get a jump on Apple's smash hit iPad. Competing Microsoft divisions conspired to kill the project, according to a former company executive writing in the *New York Times*.

There's More to Know about Culture

Professors Ken Thompson of DePaul University and Fred Luthans of the University of Nebraska have studied corporate culture in depth and put forth these seven characteristics of culture:

- **Culture Equals Behavior.** "Culture" describes the behaviors that represent the general operating norms in your environment. Culture is neither good or bad; it just "is." Note that some aspects of your firm's culture will support your success, and other aspects will stand in the way. For example, holding people accountable for performance will help you succeed. Out-of-the-park customer service will help, and so will engaging your employees. Tolerating poor performance or a lack of discipline when it comes to established processes will impede your success.

- **Culture Is Learned.** People learn from childhood to behave a certain way through positive or negative consequences that flow from what they do. Behavior that's rewarded is repeated and eventually becomes part of the culture. It is easy to forget that rewards need not be monetary. A simple thank you from a partner for work performed well can help mold the culture.

- **Interaction Plays a Key Role.** Employees learn culture by interacting with other employees. Most behaviors and rewards in firms involve other employees. An applicant quickly gets a feeling for your culture and whether it "fits"—while waiting in the reception area or during the first phone contact.

- **Sub-Cultures Meet Important Needs.** Diverse groups of employees have quite different wants and needs. Sometimes, employees value rewards that are not directly related to the behaviors partners or managers want. People can get social rewards from co-workers or have their most important needs meet on project teams.

- **People Shape the Culture.** Personalities and experiences of employees create the culture of an organization. For example, if most of the people in your firm are outgoing, the culture is likely to be open and sociable. If artifacts depicting the company's history and values are in evidence, people value their history and culture. If few closed door meetings are held, the culture tends to be unguarded. If negativity is widespread and complained about by employees, a culture of negativity will take hold—and that is particularly difficult to overcome.

- **Culture Is Negotiated.** One person cannot create a culture, nor can one person alone change it. Culture change is a process of give-and-take by all members of an organization. Formalizing strategic direction, developing systems, and establishing measurements must be owned by the group responsible for them. Otherwise, employees will not own them.

- **Culture Change Is Difficult.** Culture change requires people to change their behaviors. It is often difficult for people to unlearn their old way of doing things and to start performing the new behaviors consistently. Persistence, discipline, employee involvement, kindness and understanding, organization development work, and training can help.

How to Assess Your Firm's Culture

There are several ways firm leaders can get a clearer picture of a firm's current culture. To do it right, though, you need to try to be an impartial observer. Look at the employees and the way they interact in your firm as if you were an outsider. One option is to pretend you are an anthropologist observing a group of natives you have never seen before.

- Be an Impartial Observer:

    1. Watch for emotions, which are a clear indicator of values. People will get excited or upset about things that are important to them. Examine conflicts closely, because they can be very revealing.

    2. Observe the "natives" in their natural habitat. What objects and artifacts sit on the desks or hang on the walls? What do the common areas and furniture arrangements tell you? At one firm we know, the lobby features a ten-key adder mounted under glass, with the warning: "In case of emergency, break glass." You can bet that history matters in that firm.

    3. When you observe and interact with employees, watch for things that are not there. If nobody mentions something you think is important (like your clients), that is priceless information.

    4. Take a Culture Walk: One way to observe the culture in your organization is to take a walk around the building and look

at some of the physical signs of culture. How is the space allocated? Where are the offices located? How much space is given to whom? Where are people located?

5. What do people write to one another? What is said in memos or e-mail? What is the tone of messages (formal or informal, pleasant or hostile, etc.)? How often do people communicate with one another? Is all communication written, or do people communicate verbally? What interaction between employees do you see? How much emotion is expressed during the interaction?

- Utilize Surveys and Focus Groups:

    1. Interview or survey your employees:

        o Does your firm really "walk the walk and talk the talk" in terms of the work environment, firm culture, and staff development?

        o As illustrated in the vignette that opened this chapter, many firms conduct exit interviews with employees as a best practice, but they are already gone at that point, and anything you get from them is either sour grapes or too late to fix. Here are two alternatives:

    2. Conduct "stay interviews": Leading-edge firms interview their top talent before they ever think about leaving the firm. You are interviewing or surveying them to find out what they are happy with about the firm, what they wish was different, and what should change. The questions are similar to those asked

in an exit interview but asked before the fact, while you can still act on them. Questions that get at firm culture are best and most revealing when they are indirect. For example:

○ What would you tell a friend about our firm if he or she was about to start working here?

○ What is the one thing you would most like to change about the firm?

○ Who is a hero around here? Why?

○ What do you like best about the firm? What is your favorite characteristic?

○ What kinds of people are most likely to succeed? Which ones fail?

○ What question would you most like to ask a candidate for a job here?

One option is to use surveymonkey.com or some other electronic survey. The upside is that people can answer the questions anonymously, take the survey at their desk, and take their time thinking about the answers. The downside is that it tends to be a one-dimensional snapshot of what's on their mind at the moment and less revealing.

3. Bring together focus groups: More progressive firms are conducting focus groups, putting together people from the firm likely to encourage each other to go deeper in their

conversations. You need to be careful not to put layers of people together that will inhibit the level of trust and open conversation you need. You cannot have a partner in the room.

At one firm I worked with, a staff accountant revealed that when she was hired, she was told the firm really valued work/life balance and would allow her to work from home. But the reality was quite different. "They get angry when I work from home. I can't say anything because I like the firm and want to keep my job," she said. Others in the group nodded their heads in agreement.

On learning about this disconnect, the managing partner put together a team and asked for volunteers to brainstorm how to make things better. It made a huge difference, and the employees felt validated because what they said was acted upon.

4. Whether you have an electronic survey or use focus groups, you need to set it up so that employees will trust that what they say is not going to get them in trouble. You need to reassure people that their names are not going to show up on a report someplace and that what they write or say will be paraphrased so that it cannot be tied back to a specific individual. Finally, the partner group needs to be willing to take action on the results of the survey. It's best to include the people you are surveying so that you get employees involved in making change happen.

Moving to a Strengths-Based Culture

In a recent Gallup survey, the results show that only 17 percent of people play to their strengths in their current work environment. While most firms work hard to fix weaknesses, the reality is that we will get far better results in performance, retention, and promotion if we put more emphasis on building on the strengths of the people on our teams.

The Gallup survey also shows another interesting fact that we should sit up and take notice of—only 9 percent of employees today are truly engaged in their work performance by using their personal strengths. With all of this evidence, leaders in CPA firms must work hard to improve the current culture and the ability to identify and capitalize on the strengths of the people on their teams.

This is not just "fluff." There is neurological research by the Center for Applied Positive Psychology that supports that when people are happy and working within their strengths, they learn faster, are more receptive to coaching, and are more engaged in their firm.

A positive, or "strengths-based," firm seeks to identify what is right in people rather than correct what is wrong. It's an ingredient that is missing in most firms.

Think about the way we currently recruit, how we administer performance management and leadership development programs, and how we value certain attributes. Is the focus on what people can accomplish when stacked up against the job description, or is it what talents they possess that can be used in the firm? If you are like most firms, you concentrate on the tasks that have been built for the masses and the technical skills that they have learned. While these are certainly components of success in the firm, an individual team member's strengths are often not even considered.

Strengths are defined as "a preexisting capacity for a particular way of behaving, thinking, or feeling that is authentic and energizing to the user and enables optimal functioning, development, and performance." Notice this definition does not begin with what is best for the firm; it begins with what is best for the individual. This is a new way of thinking that we must develop over time. These strengths can include talents, skills, creativity, passions, hopes, dreams, and interests. They are individual in nature and not "cookie-cutter" in nature. These innate strengths will allow each team member in your firm to develop his or her skills and connect them with the needs of the firm.

Some "experts" state that to be a great leader in the accounting profession you must be an exceptional communicator, others say you must have a talent for relationship building, and still others insist that you must be exceptionally detailed. However, the fact is, nobody can be all of these things. You are what you are, and your innate strengths will guide your career success. You just have to know what they are and build on them.

To change the firm so that it will move in the direction of a true strengths-based culture, the firm must ensure that

- all team members are active participants in the helping process (empowerment);

- all people are willing to explore and use their individual strengths;

- the firm believes that strengths will foster the motivation for continual and ongoing growth;

- the firm will take a long-term approach to developing individual strengths and will not see it as a "Band-Aid" approach.

Once your firm makes the decision to convert their current culture to one built on strengths, development will be needed in the following areas:

- performance management

- leadership and management development

- succession planning

- recruiting

Strengths-Based Performance Management

In many firms, managers are instructed to look at an employee's challenges and weaknesses and coach for greater performance. Such assessments usually pay only cursory attention to an employee's strengths. Performance reviews and subsequent remedial programs focus almost exclusively on weaknesses.

Ignoring strengths in favor of weaknesses has a profound effect on individual performance, according to a recent Corporate Leadership Council survey of nearly twenty thousand employees in twenty-nine countries. Emphasis on performance strengths was linked to a

36 percent improvement in performance, while emphasis on performance weaknesses was linked to a 27 percent decline in performance.

What's the difference between strengths-based performance management and traditional performance management that focuses on employees' weaknesses? In the traditional system, feedback is saved as part of a periodic review. Data are collected, and performance is rated on the past. Strengths are accepted as a given, and the focus is on developing the weak areas. Goal setting is based on improving those weaknesses, and little if any attempt is made to build on strengths.

By contrast, strengths-based performance management recognizes good work and strengths. Managers offer regular feedback in real time and hold honest performance management conversations. The system differentiates between tolerable and business-critical weaknesses and manages performance expectations. Finally, it seeks to build employees' strengths and to get feedback from employees on their own performance.

Since we tend to get more frustrated by what an employee is not doing, we may fail to recognize the value that they bring to the table.

Strengths-Based Leadership and Management Development

Development has its place in a strengths-based culture as with any firm. Strengths-based firms don't ignore weaknesses, but they make weaknesses nearly irrelevant. Leaders can achieve this in three ways:

- Redefine the role so that it plays better to the person's strengths.

- Have that person partner with someone who compensates for the weaknesses.

- Assemble teams from the start based on everyone's strengths.

If all of the above fails to get the employee to perform, then managers would begin the process of the more traditional performance improvement that may ultimately lead to separation. The thought that all people fit in every job is absurd, but finding the people with the right strengths to fit a firm's needs is imperative to ultimate growth and profitability expectations.

Strengths-Based Recruiting

While a firm may first start the process of change in their firm with performance management, they must also change the process they have for recruiting individuals in order to ensure the team they build is continually strong. A firm must identify the strengths needed for the positions and then find candidates with those strengths. Redefining job descriptions with a strengths focus and using tools that will identify the correct candidates is a strong step. A few tools that you should explore include:

- The Kolbe A™ Index, www.boomer.com/kolbe

- *Now, Discover Your Strengths*, by Marcus Buckingham and Donald O. Clifton, PhD

The new recruitment process your firm develops will help the firm find people who love to do the job, not just those who simply can do the job.

Getting Started on Firm Strengths

If you want to embed strengths in your firm, the following are important first steps:

- Define strengths needed in the firm, and make sure they are tied to the business strategy.

- Start at the top by having leaders assess their strengths to get support for the concept by using the Kolbe A™ Index.

- Decide whether to roll out the program beyond top leaders by department, location, or level based on what makes sense for your firm.

- Start with performance management, leadership development, or recruitment, and master one process before moving to another.

- Be patient and continue to evaluate your approach and refine as necessary.

This cultural change is not a steamroller process; it's more of a quiet evolution. Once people start talking about strengths and relating to others based on these defined traits, you will see improvements in decision making, teamwork, supervisor-employee relationships, and employee authenticity and engagement.

Visit www.boomer.com/collaboration and download

Collaboration Tool #3

The Stay Interview

Chapter Four: Start From the Top Down

"Well, the good news is that we made decent money in the last quarter," said Tom Mitchum, pushing aside a summary report from the firm's accounting system. *"And so far this year we seem to be recovering, bit by bit, from the great recession. We're on track to grow revenue about five percent annualized." His partners, Sam Jones and Bill Templeton, nodded agreement. They were meeting in the firm's conference room.*

"Looks like our effort to touch base with our best business clients has paid off," Bill Templeton said. "At least we haven't lost anyone to the competition since Monolith left earlier this year."

Sam Jones cleared his throat. "I have news that's not that good," he said. "I finished up with the 'stay interview' project this week, and it looks like we are not the 'happy family' we'd like to think we are."

"What's the verdict?" asked Tom Mitchum. "As I said, we can't afford to lose any more good people."

"Well, to sum up the feedback I've been getting, the staff thinks we are way behind the curve when it comes to technology, and we have significant generational issues. There's almost an 'us versus them' thing going on."

"Sounds like the problems that led Tracy to look for greener pastures are not just an isolated thing." Tom said. "Give us some examples."

"On the plus side, the consensus seems to be that the firm is committed to giving people the technical training they need," Sam said. "And we do make sure everyone gets the CPE hours they need. But some of the managers say they need more leadership training and help with soft skills, like communication and business development. One of them told me she feels trapped in the role of 'right-hand' man, with no chance to learn what she needs to become a partner."

"Who said that?" Bill asked. "I bet it was Kimberly Wilson. She is a piece of work. Always has something to complain about. These young ones are not willing to pay their dues like we had to do."

"The only way I could get people to open up was to promise strict confidentiality," Sam said. "Even at that I'm not sure they were really opening up to me. In retrospect I wish we had brought in an outside consultant. We probably would have gotten more honest feedback."

"Are there other examples?" asked Tom. "What about the work/life balance issue Tracy mentioned?"

"One of our best guys—clearly future partner material—asked to work a reduced schedule after the birth of his first child, to share childcare duties with his wife," Sam said. "We wouldn't let him do that, and he's resented it ever since. He says there's a mismatch between our spoken core values and our 'real' core values that translated to our thinking that he is not loyal to the firm."

"So we are behind the curve on technology, too. How does that affect us? Can you elaborate?" Tom asked.

"You know these younger staff members don't operate in a vacuum. They talk to each other and network with peers in other firms, too," Sam

explained. "We have this patchwork quilt of audit and tax software that makes their life difficult and leads to a lot of extra work for them, especially overtime they don't get paid for.

"Other firms have invested in integrated, end-to-end software solutions that let staff get more done in less time," Sam continued. "The people over at T&B didn't log anywhere near the OT we did last season, and they get to work from anywhere there's an Internet connection."

Bill Templeton had kept quiet, but could no longer hold back. It was clear he was doing a slow burn. "I can see where this is all headed, and I don't like it. Whatever happened to proving yourself and demonstrating a work ethic? When I was coming up through the ranks, you had to put in seventy to eighty hours a week. I had to sacrifice time away from my wife and kids, too. Nobody treated me with kid gloves along the way."

Tom looked to Bill. "I feel your pain, Bill. But times have changed, and we have to move with them or get left behind. It will be tough for all of us, but it's essential, and we have to be open to new ways of running the firm."

"Here's what I think we should do," said Sam. "Let's organize a team of people, from both the audit and tax side of the practice, with different age groups and backgrounds, and let them come up with ideas about specific ways we can improve. No holds barred."

Tom nodded agreement. "Good idea, Sam. If we involve everyone from top to bottom, we're more likely to get the buy-in we need to make changes. We'll have the final say, of course. Meanwhile, Bill, why don't you look into what we need to do on the technology side of things to become more efficient and productive?"

■

All Progress Begins with the Truth

Today, firms of all sizes are grappling with the same kind of issues that partners Mitchum, Jones, and Templeton face as a firm. Most realize that their staff is the greatest asset of all and that healthy growth comes from having employees that are unified in mind, body, and spirit in supporting the firm's efforts. And many are beginning to view technology as an enabler rather than a necessary evil.

Coming to terms with internal issues before pursuing a healthy culture is an important first step. This may sound simple, but it is incredibly difficult for firms to grasp and take action on.

Over the past few years, firms have felt like they were really making progress in this area because they cut staff, and most of the staff members who got cut were individuals who were not their top performers. The remaining team members—at the staff and manager levels—are generally the most intelligent and motivated individuals that we have experienced in our industry in a long time.

The profession faces a broad range of complex issues today, ranging from succession planning—developing future firm leaders—to sustaining growth (or just staying even) during tough economic times. The toughest problem of all, though, is the growing awareness of the need to change the look and feel of our firms and the way we run our businesses to stay ahead of the curve and sustain ourselves into the future.

To my way of thinking, this requires getting away from an individual mind-set (switching from thinking "What's right for me?" to "What's right for *us*?") and building a collaborative approach rather than operating like individual pods or practices siloed within firms.

Decide What Kind of Firm You Want to Be

One bit of truth telling that needs to take place is that the partners/owners need to decide what type of firm they want. In our experience there seem to be two roads frequently traveled:

- *Shared services*, an approach in which the partners build and maintain their own book of business. They often slice the revenue pie equally after covering overheads like office space, technology, and staff support.

- *Shared vision,* where a group of partners/owners has a common company vision and goal for the firm and wants to build something greater than the sum of its parts.

In one real-world example from our practice, three partners in a fifteen-partner California firm shared a single vision: they wanted to serve clients in new ways, bundling services using an annual contract approach. The other partners preferred the status quo and would not even consider testing the idea to see if it would work. The upshot is that the three youngest, most creative, and forward-thinking partners pulled out and started their own firm.

Since the split, both firms have gone their separate ways and done reasonably well. But had the firm stayed together, growth and profitability for all concerned would have been much more impressive.

When it comes to making changes, firm leaders have a hard time evaluating their own partner group. The first step in developing a healthy firm culture and moving toward a new, collaborative business model is to let go of partners who are not supporting the changes you want to make.

There is an expression used in change-management circles: "This is a northbound train." When you have a compelling vision of who you are, what you do, and where you plan to go, those who want to ride a different train are free to do so.

When it comes to culture, most partners fit into one of the following four categories:

1. underachievers who do not care about firm culture

2. underachievers who promote firm culture

3. high achievers who do not care about firm culture

4. high achievers who promote firm culture

The goal is to eliminate the 1s (usually an easy decision) and the 3s (a much harder, but equally important decision), as depicted in Exhibit 1.

Exhibit 1: The Performance & Firm Culture Model

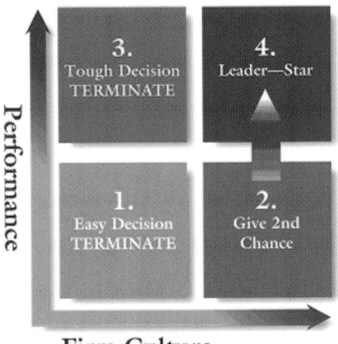

Source: *Boomer Advantage Guide to Training & Learning*

At the partner level, the problem children are the quadrant 3 individuals. However, they are not really the biggest problem. The real problem is the unwillingness of the quadrant 4 individuals to take action on removing the quadrant 3 partners.

Think about it. If you take the first step in this process and draw the above chart, plug in the names of partners, and identify the ones that are in quadrant 3, that is easy. The hard part is being honest about the issue and taking action to correct the problem. Taking action is tough but necessary for a healthy culture.

Any firm that has gone through the pain of making changes at the partner level admits that while the initial decision was not fun, the outcome was positive for both the leadership group and the firm. According to one of our clients who successfully eliminated a quadrant 3 partner, the positive results were felt throughout the firm in the very first year.

Choose Your Leadership Carefully

Firm leadership sets the tone for culture, so choose your next managing partner with care. A managing partner must be able to define a clear company vision as well as pattern a steady and sustainable work ethic. Whether the firm is in a period of rapid growth or a period of recession, the managing partner must not neglect to assess what he or she is doing to promote culture. While some partners may be productive and superb with clients, they might not be able to motivate the firm toward a common vision.

Evaluate how your managing partner feels (or would feel) about the following tasks in the firm:

- On a regular basis, have lunch or coffee with randomly chosen employees, and explore their concerns and suggestions.

- At least two days a week, walk through the office and chat with people.

- Support training efforts by attending a few sessions with staff (not just other partners).

- Set a sustainable work pace, and monitor those who tend to work excessive hours (a well-balanced workweek will significantly reduce sick days and burnout).

If your managing partner is open to these suggestions, then congratulations! The firm has a great leader in place and is on the way to building a collaborative and prosperous culture. If he or she hates these types of tasks and would rather delegate them to the firm administrator or another partner, you may be in trouble.

If a firm hopes to operate like "flying geese"—where team members line up behind and support leadership—the managing partner must care about individuals and not hold him or herself as superior. Firm employees must feel valued by leadership! A positive, highly motivated managing partner is critical to making this happen.

Build a Team that Clicks

Having a motivated team driving toward the same vision is vital to a firm's success. It is no secret that finding and developing a group of people who function as a unified group is difficult. Your firm must commit to hiring, training, and retaining the best people it can find. These "A players" are those whom you hire for their positive and contagious attitude; instilling the requisite knowledge is the easy part.

As I work with partners across the country, I regularly encounter the kind of talk we heard from Bill Templeton at the beginning of this chapter: "Employees today don't have the work ethic we had when I was starting out." My reply? "You're wrong. They may work in a different way, but they do have an amazing work ethic, but it is not the same as yours. Now get over it."

Our clients are about 50 percent right when they say, "Staff members today want balance." The other 50 percent of the equation is that partners and senior members of the staff want the same thing! Our society has taken note of the reality that there is more to life than work!

We all want more time with our friends, children, grandchildren, and outside interests. Traveling, learning new things, and having the time to develop new skills are goals that are very important in our lives. That does not diminish the fact that we also want a career that is challenging, rewarding, and provides the opportunity for multiple career paths. Let's face it—we want it all!

Therefore, successful firms build solutions into their cultures that address these concerns. These include:

- additional training

- bonus and equity opportunities

- remote access and flexible working hours

- comp time or paid time for overtime

- firm events that encourage fun and relationship building (during the work day)

- mandatory time off when the firm closes for a full week

- sabbatical programs for manager and partners

There are many ways to build an attractive culture for the team you have worked hard to develop. The career that you help your team build should be challenging, rewarding, fun, and an important *part* of a tremendous life.

Communicate the Firms' Core Values, Mission, and Plan!

Try the following experiment. Ask a partner, a manager, and an administrative assistant the following question, "What is our firm's mission, and how do you play a part in that mission?"

If your firm is like most, you will not get a consistent answer to the first part of the question, and you might get a few raised eyebrows and shrugging of shoulders on the second part. A firm's culture is only viable when employees understand the managing partner's vision and work toward it.

Here are a few steps that will increase productivity and promote culture:

- *Make sure employees establish measurable goals and understand their professional growth paths in the company.* Their goals should weave into the firm's overall vision and mission.

- *Develop open and trusting relationships with employees.* This initiative starts with the managing partner, but it applies to every partner or manager who oversees staff. One weak link can hurt the firm's collective efforts in this area. Interact with employees regularly, and offer praise or precise suggestions for improvement.

- *Evaluate employees by measurable goals.* Assess each employee's performance by goals you can measure versus the number of hours they spend in the office.

- *Get creative.* One managing partner sends out a mini newsletter to employees each week to keep them current with the firm's happenings. Another managing partner holds monthly staff meetings during which he personally gives a "state of the company" address.

Remember, culture does not just "happen"; it is cultivated and grows with time and effort. Ongoing communication is essential to cultivating a desirable culture in your firm.

Encourage Collaboration

Once the leadership is on board, the team is selected, and the plan is communicated, it is time for leadership to encourage collaboration. Here are five ways CPA firm leaders can encourage collaboration:

- **Reward People for Sharing Data and Information.** Sharing data and information internally creates value by harnessing resources across the organization. Too often firms are siloed in a way that is detrimental to the kind of cooperation and collaboration that can deliver value to clients. Annual performance reviews (from the top down) should include an evaluation of how team members share data and information to create value for the firm and its clients.

- **Avoid Pitting People against Each Other.** The pyramid structure of most firms and the "up or out" approach create internal competition that can easily become unhealthy. One option to consider is harnessing complementary skills by encouraging cross-functional teams to meet project challenges.

- **Recognize People for Gaining Broad Input.** Successful collaborative organizations create value by recognizing leaders for gaining broad input into decisions. When its leaders make decisions in a vacuum, the firm suffers. Worse yet, we've seen some partners make shoot-from-the-hip decisions without analyzing adequate data and information and without input from others. The firm benefits when people participate in decisions regardless of level, role, or region.

- **Change the Conversation.** Language is a powerful component of organizational culture. Too often, shop talk includes sports metaphors and internally competitive language. As a leader, encourage your team to change the conversation and embrace collaborative language. In a collaborative organization, you will hear language like: "Let's get input from sales" or "We can make a better decision if we engage finance to run the numbers" or "Let's connect now with corporate communications to see how different approaches to solving this problem will affect our reputation."

- **Clarify the Role of Competition.** Team members need to know when to compete and when to collaborate. Educate your managers and staff that competition belongs in the marketplace, not in the workplace.

Build a Support Network

Good firms may learn from the first five lessons and make some progress in building a suitable firm culture. *Great* firms, however, enlist a support network and/or a consultant to engineer a world-class firm culture.

Conducting a firm summit is a strategy that many firms use to establish and reinforce cultural values. A great consultant is not only a facilitator but also a coach who will tell you the truth—even when it hurts a little!

Once a vision and cultural values are confirmed, enlist a group of peers to help the firm build confidence and maintain momentum. Peer networking is an indispensable part of doing business. Having a support network of like-minded firms could make the difference between incremental and exponential growth.

Firm culture is an evolutionary process; one can't merely speak it into existence. Follow the lessons outlined above, and give everyone in the organization a reason to feel good about the future. Remember, no one strategy fits every firm because all begin at different places. However, every firm can experience success by facing challenges head on; choosing a visionary leader; selecting type "A" staff; communicating effectively; and building a support system.

Visit www.boomer.com/collaboration and download

Collaboration Tool #4

The Firm Leader Upward Evaluation

Chapter Five: Continue From the Inside Out

"Well, that was truly embarrassing," said Tom Mitchum, managing part-ner at Mitchum, Jones & Templeton LLC, as he sank into a plush chair in the firm's paneled conference room.

"What happened?" asked partner Sam Jones, in the act of pouring his third cup of coffee of the morning. *"You don't rattle that easily."*

"You know we've had problems with strangers coming into the office—and just the other day someone walked off with one of our laptops," Tom said. *"So just a few minutes ago a young twenty-something woman walked past my office, and I chased after her down the hall. I thought maybe she'd snuck past the reception area."*

Sam leaned forward in his chair. "Was she up to no good?" he asked.

"I came up behind her and tapped her on the shoulder. She looked at me with that deer-in-the-headlights look," Tom continued. *"I asked who she was, and she said, Mary Schmidt, from the tax department."*

"Then what happened?"

"It became really awkward," Tom said through a sheepish grin. *"I mum-bled an apology and said something like, 'You must be one of the new people.' She said, 'No, sir…I've been here ninety days."*

Sam laughed and so did Bill Templeton, who'd entered the room during the conversation, just in time to hear the punch line.

"Sounds like you need to get out from behind the desk," Bill said. "That might be reasonable if this was a big firm, but we just have one office and forty people. No wonder we've got an 'us versus them' thing going on with the managers and staff."

"It is certainly a wake-up call," Tom admitted. "And all the more reason for us to continue working on changing the culture here and building a better work environment."

"It starts with us, of course," Sam said. "We have to start behaving differently ourselves, setting the right example, and changing the tone. Not that I think we should build a bonfire, hold hands, and sing 'Kumbaya.'"

"Of course not; that wouldn't be billable," Tom said and smiled. "But make a note of that for the next office picnic."

■

Although fictionalized for dramatic effect, the incident reported above actually took place while I was visiting with the managing partner at a forty-person, single-office firm. It is an excellent way to illustrate three important points:

- In order for change to occur, someone has to start behaving differently.

- The effort to build internal collaboration and a good team starts at the top.

- Internal collaboration becomes the glue that holds the firm together/bridges the gap between leadership and employees (us and them).

Although many people in the accounting profession say that change is necessary, that doesn't make it easy or fast. In fact, much of the behavior in firms today may be detrimental to meaningful change. After all, "the way we've always done things around here" is generally more comfortable, compelling—and less risky—than the potential reward of the future.

Technology, the economic model, demographics, increased regulation, and client expectations are just a few of the areas in which firms face rapid change. The ability to implement change in a positive manner has become both a professional practice and a skill set of great value to today's firms.

It's really important to understand that the future of our profession and your firm hinges on being open to change and new ways of conducting business. It all starts with a frank and honest discussion among the partners or shareholders. You need to talk about what is working well in your firm and what is not.

True leaders need to be willing to let go. But what I find is that in many firms the managing partner is holding the reins too tight. They may say things like, "I want people to come up with new ideas or new ways of doing things." But if they are approached with an idea or a group of people who want to work together on a project, what they hear is, "That won't work because…" or "If we have three people on that project, it will cost too much, so let's have only one person on it."

The unintended result is that people walk away demoralized, become unwilling to step forward, and often start looking elsewhere. I've watched many firms lose really good partners or potential partners because their ideas were stepped on this way. Invariably the reaction when someone leaves is "They didn't fit in here," despite the fact that they moved on to another firm—or started one on their own—and became very successful.

The old way of running a firm is not wrong, by any means, but the new way is so much better for everyone. Rather than the classic "up or out" pyramid structure, we will see a flatter structure to firms in the future. There will be teams of people doing client work together and collaboratively finding better solutions—and additional services—for clients, rather than a partner or senior making all the decisions. Plus, if one person on the team retires or leaves, clients will not panic, because they have strong relationships with several others. Another benefit is that the team approach makes it more difficult for someone who strikes off on their own to take clients with them.

In firms that are truly collaborative, we will see ideas developed by a group of people from inception rather than "lone rangers" who operate alone and have to sell their ideas. The group will support and nurture the idea by bringing in other team members as needed to make the idea better. The thought process is: "Let's sit at the table and figure this out—together."

By pulling together everyone's ideas, thoughts, and intellectual capital, the firm will benefit from "group think" rather than "individual think." There will be little room for individual egos in this environment. Silos within the firm will deteriorate, and power teams will emerge. Accepting the fact that a group approach is better than a competitive, "me"-oriented approach will go a long way toward making the change to a more collaborative workforce.

Another benefit to changing from a traditional model to a collaborative one is the impact it will have on recruiting and retaining the best and the brightest. Firms today have a reputation for being predominantly male, white, and aging at the partner level; female, middle-aged, and white at the manager level; and slightly more diverse in race, gender, and nationality at the staff level.

Given the changing demographics of our country today and the reality that our younger leaders have a more diverse and global outlook of the world, it is safe to say that the "look" of our firms is already changing. And it is a welcome change for future firm leaders who have gone to school and often traveled the world with friends of different nationalities and cultures.

Our younger professionals have grown up collaborating, and now they expect it when they enter firms. This group of people has been programmed from their growing-up years to care for their community and others. Think about the youth of today and how they are taught, motivated, and rewarded in schools to care for their community and work with their classmates on projects. They will never be satisfied in their work life not using these skills to develop a sense of purpose and dedication for the overall firm and team, not just themselves.

Create a Talent Blueprint

During exit interviews, one of the first things people always tell me is that they left because the firm didn't make them feel important, didn't care about them, and never talked to them. If you want people to stay with your firm, you have to get them involved in projects that use their strengths and make them feel important.

The first step in building a collaborative structure internally is to start with a talent blueprint of each person in the firm, and use that information to plug people in where they belong and will most likely succeed. It's important to get the right people on the bus rather than just bring people in and put them to work in an arbitrary way.

Here's an all-too-common conversation with a new hire: "Oh, you are going to be a staff accountant. Here is your job description, and here are the steps you need to take along the way to become a manager, and here is the CPE you need to take." At some firms, that is literally the end of the conversation—as long as they do what the job description requires and stay current with CPE, the staff and management are done talking.

To build a collaborative, strengths-based culture, you have to look at more than just technical ability. Find out what people are good at, and capitalize on that. Of course you have to pay attention to technical skills, what your people know, and the experience they have. CPE is very important, but it is not the only thing that matters. There are other important issues to address as part of the talent blueprint:

- **Career goals.** What do they want to achieve in their career? Do they want to go deeper in their career or broader? Do they want to start going up the ladder and become a leader in the future? How about a lateral move, like climbing a lattice?

- **Personality traits.** If they are extroverted, don't put them in the back room, chained to a keyboard, because you will lose them in a heartbeat. Alternatively, don't force an introverted person into the wrong role. Don't make him or her speak at the next Rotary luncheon. Instead, recognize that he or she is more likely to excel in small groups. Or, send him or her to a client to work side-by-side with someone in their office.

- **How they like to work.** Some people really prefer detail work, while others are more satisfied when things are more organized and methodical. Perhaps you have a visionary "idea person" who is not all that detail oriented and likes to come up with big ideas. The more you can get in touch with how you like to work and live your life, the better off you will be.

Those of us who are baby boomers may think of this as a lot of "fluff" or handholding—something our superiors never did for us. But the fact is up-and-coming talent in the profession want their leaders to ask, "What can we do to make the workplace better? What will it take to keep you engaged in the firm? What would push you to leave? What do you really want in terms of your career?"

The rising generations have had so much help and guidance through-out their lives that now these younger professionals expect someone will help guide them to make the right decisions in the workplace. They're smarter and more diverse and well rounded than we ever were, but they are used to working in a very collaborative workforce. Leadership is going to have to help young professionals get to where they need to be.

As you profile your current team, you should begin to look critically at the skills that are not in your firm today. Are you a firm that is full of research-oriented people, but the number of process-orient-ed project leaders is thin? Or, do you have a firm full of introverted followers who take direction well, but not many individuals who are hungry to "own" responsibilities and want to lead initiatives in the firm?

After you analyze your current situation, you must prepare to look beyond the technical needs of today and to focus on the leadership needs of the future. Firms absolutely need skills and abilities, but they also need emotional intelligence. This will require analysis, new hiring skills, and a dedication to changing old habits. Remember, if you continue to hire, promote, and motivate the way you have in the past, you will get the same talent you have had in the past, and that will not be good enough in the future.

Putting together the leadership of the future requires that you look at each person as a separate and unique individual—identifying the unique characteristics that her or she has and allowing him or her to develop those skills. Just because someone is not the best business developer does not mean he or she is not valuable; one may indeed have a gift for putting processes in place that will save the firm hours in productivity and efficiency. Another person—a superb business developer—may not like to research new systems. A good leader will see that this person's motivation will come from front-stage projects dealing with client and prospect interactions. One is not wrong or less valuable; both are equally amazing.

A positive way to find out what is floating around in your future leaders' minds is to form a "Tomorrows Leaders Initiative" in your firm. Give them objectives, but let them figure out the strategies, ideas, and timelines for initiatives that will help the firm prepare for the future. Build a team that is cross-generational and cross-functional. Choose a leader who is not a current partner. Consider rotating leaders throughout the year, because changing leadership quarterly will give others the opportunity to lead, keep the group moving, and force them to work as a team.

Have them talk about the hard issues: work/life balance, work ethics, customer/client service, remote work arrangements, technology, training and development, and succession. These are all topics that each generation should address to capture their views on the issues and what they would do to collaborate on solutions.

Take a Deeper Look at Strengths

If you are like most firms, you concentrate on the tasks that have been built for the masses and the technical skills that they have learned. While these are certainly a component of success in the firm, individual team member's strengths are often not even considered. At most firms, managers are instructed to look at an employee's challenges or "need work" areas and then to coach for improvement. Remedial programs typically focus only on weaknesses.

Ignoring strengths in favor of weaknesses has a profound effect on individual performance, however. A 2002 Corporate Leadership Council survey of nearly twenty-thousand employees in twenty-nine countries found that an emphasis on performance strengths was linked to a 36 percent improvement in performance, while emphasis on performance weaknesses was linked to a 27 percent decline in performance.

Please take note that strengths-based firms don't ignore weaknesses, but they make weaknesses nearly irrelevant. Leaders can achieve this in three ways:

- Redefine the role so that it plays better to the person's strengths.

- Have that person partner with someone who compensates for the weaknesses.

- Assemble teams from the start based on everyone's strengths.

If all of the above fail to get the employee to perform, then managers should begin the process of the more traditional performance improvement that may ultimately lead to separation. The thought that all people fit in every job is absurd, but finding the people with the right strengths to fit a firm's needs is imperative to ultimate growth and profitability expectations.

The Kolbe Wisdom™—The Ultimate Team Development Tool

Want a tool that can help and is statistically proven to build successful teams, hire individuals that fit a firm's culture, develop leaders for the future, and motivate and retain current staff as well as resolve conflict?

The Kolbe Wisdom™ is a psychological system developed by well-known theorist Kathy Kolbe. It emerged from her scientific studies (starting in 1970) of behavioral differences among people. In the 1980s, Kolbe used what she discovered from her research to advise such business giants as Kodak, IBM, Xerox, and Alaska Airlines.

The underlying premise of Kolbe's work is that people who work according to their instincts accomplish more. Those who fight or work against their instincts suffer stress (the most common workplace malady) and often fail to reach peak performance. Developed nearly thirty years ago, this system has been proven 96 percent accurate in test-retest reliability.

Kolbe System Tools	
Kolbe A	Reflects individual instinctive drive
Kolbe B	Reflects the individual's view of instinctive traits that are needed and expected in his or her current job responsibilities
Kolbe C	Reflects the supervisor's view of the instinctive traits that are needed and expected in the position being evaluated
Kolbe Team Reports	Team reports are developed from the Kolbe A, B, and C reports to show the viability and potential productivity of the team being evaluated

The Kolbe System™ maintains that creative instincts drive people to take specific actions. This mental drive is separate and distinct from passive feelings and thoughts. Creative instincts are manifested in an innate pattern that determines one's unique method of operation. We see these instinctive actions at work every day within our firms. Because they function at the subconscious level, however, we sometimes don't recognize them when evaluating someone's performance.

Instinctive behavioral patterns govern the actions, reactions, and interactions of each individual. They also determine how an individual will use his or her time and communicate. Understanding and exercising control over these instincts offers one the freedom to be functionally authentic in his or her job role.

The accounting industry is struggling with identifying, retaining, and motivating employees. Kolbe's tools are built to confront these exact challenges. But why is a tool used successfully in many other industries just now finding its way to ours? The answer is simple: we in the accounting industry are often late adopters because we want to know *exactly* what we are getting into before we jump!

Conative Instincts—The Core of the Kolbe System

Most of us don't understand our instincts. We don't learn about them in school, and they are often overlooked by human resource professionals during job interviews. A thorough exploration of all three parts of the mind is critical when we select, retain, coach, and build teams within our firms. These are:

- Cognitive (Thinking)—When we examine a résumé or identify someone's skills for a certain job, we note the cognitive skills of that person. This part of the mind has been "fed" in classrooms and by life experiences.

- Affective (Feeling)—The values and beliefs that drive a person's feelings and motivation are what make up his or her affective behaviors. These are often identified by good interview questions or tests such as the Meyers Briggs (www.meyersbriggs.com) or Predictive Index (www.piworldwide.com).

- Conative (Doing)—The energy we expend when doing work according to our instincts is conative. In its simplest form, conation is purposeful intention to act—the innate mode in which one strives toward a goal using his or her intrinsic "knack" for getting things done. This may sound foreign, but that is exactly why it is so important. It is the missing link to peak performance.

You may be thinking that since you only took one psychology class, the concept of conation will never make sense. Well, let me assure you that the Kolbe system is simple to administer, and its results are easy to track and understand. It identifies four areas of instinct:

- The "Fact Finder" instinct reveals a need to conduct in-depth investigation.

- The "Follow Thru" instinct compels us to seek a sense of order or structure.

- The "Quick Start" instinct is the force behind experimentation.

- The "Implementor" instinct takes ideas and makes them real.

Every person has a strength in each of the four areas. No style is wrong—the important thing is to help people work according to their instincts. The more people work with their strengths, the more productive they will be. They also tend to have better job satisfaction and stay with firms. A happy, productive staff member who enjoys working for your firm—sounds pretty good, doesn't it?

Suppose you have a new staff accountant hired for the tax area. The department supervisor (Kolbe Index 9-8-1-3) has always followed a tried and true process. His profile reveals a strong inclination to conduct in-depth research, devise a plan, and stick with it. There is certainly nothing wrong with that, but the new staff accountant has a very different Kolbe Index (5-8-8-2). She reviews and edits details, creates processes, and looks for new solutions. Her work style should bring a new facet to the team in the tax department. However, if the supervisor is not privy to her Kolbe Result, he will expect her to act in the same way he does. When she doesn't, he will be disappointed, she will be discouraged, and the likelihood of success will diminish.

Kolbe also has several other advantages:

- **Predict team performance.** The Kolbe System also takes individual results and melds them into reports that predict team viability and long-term success. Identifying those willing and able to work as a unified team is critical to a firm's future. Consider a firm that has assigned committees to drive tax, audit, marketing, and executive initiatives. If these groups are comprised entirely of "Fact Finders," you may well end up with "analysis paralysis." A team that complements one another via Kolbe measurements adds diversity, moves projects forward, and fosters enhanced productivity.

- **Motivate and retain.** We often associate motivation with benefits such as massages, flex time, and PTO. While these perks can be somewhat helpful, the best method to motivate and ultimately retain staff members is to help them work in instinctual, satisfying ways. Kolbe Index Results offer compelling insights that heighten self-awareness and motivate individuals to work within their unique styles.

- **Consider how you work.** Do you dig into the details of a project and find all the answers before you make a decision? Are you someone who works in chaos and generates new ideas and products? What if you could work exactly the way you feel most comfortable most of the time? Working within your instinctive behaviors is far more sustainable—and fulfilling—than "manufactured" motivation brought on by short-term benefits.

- **Develop leaders for the future.** While succession planning is on almost every firm's list, motivating and developing up-and-coming stars is not as easy as it was in the past. In order to secure a firm's future, emerging leaders must understand their unique strengths and how to capitalize on them. Second, they must know how to develop a team to implement their ideas and carry out the firm's vision. Kolbe Indexes can accurately predict how someone will lead. One index may be more suitable for one leadership role over another, depending on the makeup of the firm and where it is headed in the future.

- **Resolve conflict.** Conflict can be healthy if handled in an environment that fosters open communication. Kolbe's "Conflict CounterActives" and their A to A Comparison report identify the root issues in a conflict and offer resolution strategies. The counteractive is a positive way to facilitate a difficult process. Each side works together to explore why the conflict is occurring, how it is affecting productivity, and how to resolve the situation with mutual respect.

This tool will change your firm's culture. It's not just a feel-good test that sits in a drawer, never to be used for anything purposeful. Rather, it acts to shape your team into a productive powerhouse!

Communicate Well

To become truly collaborative, a CPA firm needs to really communicate well, and as a profession we are not really as good at that as we should be. Leaders in firms have got to learn how to sit there and have a real conversation. That is just not happening in a lot of cases.

There needs to be more training on how to have meaningful conversations. From the top down, firms need more meetings, not less—not five-hour staff meetings, but quick hits and good conversations. There needs to be a lot more internal sharing going on, not just celebrations over new clients but information on how the firm is doing financially, what the vision is or where the firm is in terms of core values, and whether the firm is living the vision/values.

Please note that if you are talking about core values and see a smirk on someone's face in the audience, you want to have a conversation with them later. It might go like this: "Let's talk. When we were talking about work/life balance, I noticed your body language. I am really interested in what you have to say because you're reaction tells me you are not feeling that core value. What are we not doing that we need to do?"

Those are the kind of open honest, sharing conversations that have to happen, and they are just not taking place. Most firms have not made progress for decades on some of this stuff. Having deep conversations with people is essential. Don't just find out what's wrong, but figure out how the firm should fix it. That is really imperative as we go forward.

Alignment of Talents and Positions

The need for open and forthright conversation becomes even clearer when the talent profile reveals that people are in the wrong positions. The first thing to do is have a conversation with them. Let's assume that you look at your pool of tax managers and find one that is extremely outgoing, loves working on multiple projects, and likes to build business but hates the detail work involved in doing tax returns.

Certainly you could use technology to automate the grunt work and streamline the process—many firms have implemented end-to-end software solutions that make life easier. But a person like that is going to feel trapped and underutilized no matter what you do on the technology side.

Better: Have a conversation and review what you have learned as a result of testing. Start out by saying, "Here are the things we have learned about you—the things you love to do. How can we transition you, and what does your job look like ten years down the road if you were doing exactly what you want to be doing? How would you build your career here?"

Based on an open dialog, you might suggest that over time his role might expand so that while still in the tax department he can bring in business and do client relationship work and come up with ideas around tax strategies and planning. A team would support him, and he would feed them the detail work. That way, the team would do the work they like to do (detail), and so would he.

The conversation ends this way: "Of course we cannot simply flip a switch to make this happen, but we can get you there. It will take time, but meanwhile let's get you the training you need and find you a mentor to help with the soft skills you need to do business development."

When I speak of conversations, what I mean is coaching, mentoring, teaching, sharing intellectual capital, and getting younger professionals engaged and involved sooner rather than later. In the "good old days," you had to do grunt work for five years or so before you would ever be turned loose with a client. The thinking was that you had to learn the work before you could go out and sell it and represent the firm.

Some say its different today, and the "young 'uns" are impatient and want to move faster. Well, maybe. But I'll bet that if most partners had been asked five years earlier if they would like to go out and get business, they would have agreed in a heartbeat. They were just never given the opportunity. That is the real difference now—we have to create the opportunities and let people move faster. The reasons will become clear in the next chapter, when we discuss collaborating with clients.

Visit www.boomer.com/collaboration and download

Collaboration Tool #5

Building a Talent Blueprint

Chapter Six: Collaborating with Clients

Sam Jones had a spring in his step and a grin on his face as he stepped into Tom Mitchum's office. The MJ&T managing partner spun around in his chair, secretly grateful for any interruption that took him away from spreadsheet hell.

"Well, you look like the cat that swallowed the canary, Sam…What's up?"

Sam dropped into a side chair. "You know I've been skeptical about the changes we've been making around here," he confessed. "But something has happened that turned me into a believer."

Tom leaned forward. "I'm happy to hear that, Sam. Tell me more."

"A couple weeks ago, I took Alex and Sally along on a visit to Ajax Construction to introduce them as part of our new client service team approach. And just like you said, I made sure they knew the meter was off and we were there to learn more about their business, what they were up against, and how we might help."

"How did Ajax react?" Tom asked. "Did they like the idea?"

"We met with the CFO and his team. They seemed pleased that we took the effort to go see them, of course. But here's the kicker: After a bit of back-and-forth, they told us something we would not have known a

thing about. The state tax people had just assessed a use tax of fifty thousand dollars on two pieces of equipment they use for excavating."

"A lot of states are getting aggressive on sales and use tax these days," Tom said and nodded. "What happened? Go on…"

Sam continued, "Alex jumped in and asked how they use the equipment. It turns out Ajax uses a conveyor and some screening contraption to take the tree roots, rocks, and debris out of the dirt so they can sell it as topsoil at a much higher price. Sally said it sounded to her like a manufacturing process, since Ajax changed the form of the dirt, and that would make the equipment exempt."

"You should have seen the CFO's eyes light up when she said that! They asked us for help convincing the state that Ajax manufactures dirt—and I just got word that the state rescinded the sales tax. We just saved the client fifty thousand dollars plus interest and penalties!"

Tom clapped his hands together, applauding. "And all because we took the effort to find out more about their business and see if we could help. That is just great news."

Sam turned a bit serious. "I have to confess something. I don't think I would ever have thought of that on my own. Look what getting those two young ones involved has done for us. Ajax loves us now."

Tom nodded. "Any maybe Sally would like to become involved in building a SUTA practice for us. That kind of creativity needs an outlet."

■

You know by now that Mitchum Jones & Templeton is a fictional CPA firm, but the facts in the collaborative example above are absolutely true. They are taken from a real-life case study illustrating creative solutions for clients of WithumSmith + Brown, the firm based in Princeton, New Jersey, that's probably best known for its viral "flash mob" videos that put to rest the notion that CPAs don't know how to have fun.

WS+B has found success in collaborating externally with clients, but they have also found success through internal innovative collaboration. In December 2011, some 150 members of the firm, from partners to staff, boarded a Manhattan-bound "R" Train in Secaucus, New Jersey, and started dancing to LMFAO's hit "Party Rock Anthem," led by Managing Partner and CEO Bill Hagaman.

Among the dancers: Senior Marketing Coordinator Sarah Cirelli, who pulled the project together along with Creative Manager Jin Young Park. Cirelli, who's certified in Zumba dance fitness, choreographed the dance moves and posted instructional videos on the firm's YouTube channel.

Visible in the background: Leonard H. Smith, CPA, who founded the firm in 1974 and has seen it grow to fourteen offices in the mid-Atlantic area, as well as Colorado and Florida. The Top 100 firm is ranked number two in the Large Firm Category on *Accounting Today*'s list of Best Firms to Work For.

As reported at the time in *Accounting Today*, Hagaman called the video shoot and six weeks of practice leading up to it "a huge team-building exercise. You can see the energy and the excitement." Rhonda

Maraziti, director of marketing and practice growth, added that "the free spirit showcased in WS+B's videos is reflective of the firm itself.

"We foster an open, creative, innovative environment and an open-door policy in general," Maraziti explained. "You're free to share thoughts and opinions, and the management and CEO are open to hearing what staff has to say, absolutely following through on suggestions to improve the firm. Because of that, the staff is happy."

Rhonda Maraziti,
director of marketing
WithumSmith + Brown
www.withum.com
Princeton, New Jersey

WS+B leverages the creativity and innovation of its people into collaborative relationships with clients as well, working alongside them as a true partner to help them grow and thrive, says partner and management committee member Jim Bourke, CPA, CITP. "We collaborate with clients on everything from tax planning and strategies to audit engagements and business operating issues," he says.

Jim Bourke
WithumSmith + Brown
www.withum.com
Princeton, New Jersey

Helping that contractor client sell dirt is just one of many examples. Bourke shared this more recent one: "The state of New Jersey allows technology companies to sell their Net Operating Losses [NOLs] for cash, as a way to raise capital," he says. "Public utilities will buy those NOLs for eighty cents on the dollar to reduce their tax liabilities. It becomes a 'win-win' for both parties." Of course, WS+B helps those transactions come to pass, earning praise and adding value in the process.

Moving Beyond "Trusted Advisor"

As we mentioned back in chapter one, a recent nationwide survey of client satisfaction conducted by CCH suggests that roughly one in three clients would move to a new CPA firm, and the primary reason they'd get the "itch to switch" is a failure on the part of the firm to regularly check in with them on their changing needs.

Forging tighter bonds with clients—collaborating with them—is a solution that adds more value. To our way of thinking, it moves beyond the "trusted advisor" role that has for years been the Holy Grail of professional service firms. Look at it this way: most people turn to someone they trust when faced with a business problem—and of course you are in an excellent position to help them solve it.

But what if they don't know there's a problem or are blind to it? What if it hits them out of the blue? Doesn't the problem-solution construct often lead to putting out fires that could have been prevented if you'd been "in the loop" earlier on? A collaborative approach gets you involved earlier, helps you understand what the client needs and where they want to be in the future, and makes it easier to help them get there.

Firms that are doing the best job of collaborating with clients are no longer following the old "hours multiplied by dollars" approach to billing, especially since we are in a results-based economy now, not an effort-based economy.

One good example is the Lawhorn CPA Group Inc. in Knoxville, Tennessee. The firm brands and packages its services using a pick-and-choose menu approach that may include accounting, tax, or strategic business consulting, based on the client's need. The firm writes an engagement letter than defines the scope and bills a fixed fee over a twelve-month period.

"We were scared to death when we first did this in 2003," says CEO Jeff Lawhorn." But in our first year, we grew firm revenue forty percent." In the beginning, the firm offered package pricing to individual clients, but business owners started clamoring for the same kind of deal, Lawhorn said in *First Choice*, a CCH online newsletter.

Jeff Lawhorn, CEO
Lawhorn CPA Group Inc.
www.lawhorncpa.com
Knoxville, Tennessee

In an interview for this book, Jeff's son and managing partner, Jason Lawhorn, picked up the story thread, describing the firm's most recent development, The Virtual Financial Office™. This package lets a small business outsource accounts payable, accounts receivable, bank reconciliation, cash and asset management, payroll, and technology to Lawhorn.

Jason Lawhorn,
managing partner
Lawhorn CPA Group Inc.
www.lawhorncpa.com
Knoxville, Tennessee

"We are changing our business model, moving away from the traditional approach of providing monthly financial statements to putting real-time systems in place so that clients can see where they are at and make real-time decisions," Jason says. "We are a proactive part of that process—moving away from independence and closer to advocacy for our clients."

Technology is the real enabler. In the "old days," only large companies with deep pockets could afford to implement dashboards and data mining, but prices have fallen, and cloud-based solutions are much more affordable. "We pull those technologies together so clients can see what is going on in real time, and we can advise them in the moment of need, not after the fact," says Jason.

For example: The owner of a personal training company with locations in Tennessee and Georgia also works internationally. She is always on the go, and things could not get done. Lawhorn put a solution together that made her managers more accountable by taking over all the day-to-day transaction processing. "A dashboard app on her iPad keeps the owner up to date on exactly what her cash levels are, what her A/R and collections look like, as well as her A/P," Jason says.

"To get this project done required a lot of collaboration, and from a time perspective, we no doubt went in the hole, but now that it is up and running, it is insanely profitable," Jason says. As mentioned, all Lawhorn engagements are value priced; while this changeover took extra time, overall what the firm invoices and collects is generally in premium mode compared to the time involved.

"We still keep time, because it provides some accountability and allows you to see, from a produced-invoiced-collected scenario, what we would have gotten if we had billed hourly," Lawhorn says. "We can see that we are at premium on a project or at budget or have had engagement creep. But because of the way salaries work, that doesn't necessarily mean we lost money. Our labor cost is generally about a third of the billing."

What's the payoff? Realization rates at Lawhorn are way up over 100 percent, Jason says. In terms of growth, nearly every year since 2003 had been in double digits, and at the time of this writing, 2012 looked like it would come in at about 12.5 percent, Jason says. "Going to a more truly collaborative approach and doing back office work for clients has made a big difference."

"Creative Destruction" at Work

"Creative destruction" is part of the DNA at Kennedy and Coe LLC, an *Accounting Today* Top 100 Firm with eight offices spread across Kansas and Colorado. "That means being willing to get rid of what doesn't work in order to do things in a better way," says the firm's CEO, Kurt Siemers, CPA, in an article that first appeared in CCH *Partners* magazine.

End-to end-paperless processing is one example of adopting a more profitable process, he says. So is what the firm calls its "value creation process," which has triggered double-digit revenue growth for the firm from clients who have made the switch away from hourly billing.

Kurt Siemers, CPA, CEO
Kennedy and Coe LLC
www.kcoe.com
Wichita, Kansas

About 50 percent of the firm's A, B, and C clients now have annual value creation agreements that cover all the services they receive during the year, from audits to tax returns or strategic planning, Siemers says. "It's all-inclusive, and they pay a fixed price, according to terms and payment schedules we establish before they sign."

The early adopters have increased fee growth for the firm by about 24 percent, Siemers says. He shares this example: "Client A and B both generate $100,000 in revenue in year one. Client A, where we followed the value creation process, increased fees to $128,000 in year two. Fees for Client B, who does not follow the process, increased fees to $104,000 in year two." Key point: that 24 percent differential has been sustainable, despite the economic downturn.

Historical data in the firm's practice management software helps forecast the price of projects in advance, Siemers says. "Our in-house scheduling system works together with practice management to generate estimates based on standard rates," he says. "Project profitability reports give us real-time reports of profitability by client so we can monitor projects to ensure that they stay profitable.

"It is a foundational change. We needed to figure out what the value is to the client and how long it will take to complete the projects," Siemers says.

A final ingredient is technology that enables streamlined and efficient operations. "I don't know how we could get our work done without having gone paperless," Siemers says. "Forty years ago when I started, we typed all the returns, and a long one ran to five pages. Today we have tax returns with one thousand pages. You can't be in business anymore without technology that gets the job done."

Greg Davis, the firm's resident IT guru, seconded that in an interview for this book. "Our newer staff has grown up collaborating, from texting to i-chatting to social media," he says. "As the next generation of clients come into ownership, collaboration will become even more important."

Greg Davis, IT director
Kennedy and Coe LLC
www.kcoe.com
Wichita, Kansas

Kennedy and Coe has improved collaboration within the firm and with clients using Microsoft Link, for example. "You can look at someone else's desktop while instant messaging and chatting," Davis says. In addition, partners, managers, and seniors at the eight-office firm all have video conferencing available right on the desktop.

"We've had video conferencing capability for eight years now, but now you no longer have to go down the hall to a conference room. That has cut way down on the need to travel. A lot more clients have better technology and infrastructure, so we can teleconference with them as well," says Davis.

His advice: "When it comes to changing technologies or adding new solutions that promote collaboration, it's important to ensure that it is easy to use. Otherwise people will just go back to what they were doing, like picking up the phone or meeting face-to-face. It has to be as easy as picking up your TV remote."

"The Navy SEALs of Accounting"

Robert L. Siegfried Jr., CPA launched The Siegfried Group LLP back in 1988 after seven years at a national firm. At age twenty-nine, he hung up a shingle in Wilmington, Delaware, looking to make accounting more challenging and interesting. "We started out as financial advisors, helping companies look forward and strategize, because talking about what was going to happen next year and helping forecast cash and profit got more attention at the top and made us more relevant and collaborative with clients," Siegfried says.

Robert L. Siegfried, CPA, founder
The Siegfried Group LLP
www.siegfriedgroup.com
Wilmington, Delaware

The strategy worked and took a quantum leap in 1995 when DuPont called asking for help with a multimillion-dollar carve out. Siegfried lined up a dozen staff to work inside the company and called it an "aha!" moment. "The client said, 'I don't need you; I just need your staff. I'll run it myself, and we will have less project risk, it will get done faster, and it will be more cost-effective.'"

At the same time, those twelve staff people were saying, "This is great! I don't like auditing, but I am working hand to hand, collaboratively, on a big problem DuPont has, and I am feeling really valued." That was the birth of Siegfried Group's Accounting Resource Service practice, where the firm puts staff into big companies to work directly for the client. Clients handle the review piece and sign-offs, taking Siegfried and his managers out of the picture. "That is significant because it elevates the role and importance of what the younger staff are doing," he says.

By 2003 the traditional side of the practice—financial advisory services, forecasting, and tax planning, mostly—was doing about $5 million. The Accounting Resource Service (ARS) practice brought in $12.5 million. "Before I knew it, we had expanded nationally and hit $73 million in revenue," Siegfried says. At that time he sold 90 percent of the firm's traditional clients to focus on ARS. It continued to flourish, reaching $86 million until a 2008 nosedive, when revenue dropped to $38 million.

Siegfried hires people with five or six years of experience, offering five main benefits: (1) interesting and challenging work, (2) enhanced marketability, (3) a great culture, (4) top end compensation, and (5) a compelling business structure averaging 35 percent growth year over year.

"We dip our staff in all different kinds of projects and turn them into the Navy SEALs of accounting," he says. "It's very attractive to younger people. They get to roll up the sleeves and get experiences they would not have the opportunity to get otherwise."

Another "aha!" moment for Siegfried centered on the realization that those young people aren't going to stay with the firm forever, and what they really care about most is future marketability. "I'm like a college president. You hate to see your best students graduate, but life changes and they move on. They meet Mr. or Mrs. Right, buy a dog, buy a house, have children, or all of the above. At some point they come in and say, 'I like working at this client, it's fifteen minutes from my house, and they've made me an offer.' We figure on getting about five years from new hires—it's like an accounting residency."

Siegfried professionals move from one industry to another at cycles of about six to nine months, building on knowledge gained from prior assignments. The variety of assignments helps them figure out what they are best at and "what they really want when they grow up," Siegfried says. In five years, most gain about ten years of experience, he says.

Siegfried agrees that the world is evolving and the accounting profession needs to change along with it. "Firms need to find a way to make things more interesting, challenging, and flexible," he says. Just one example is changing assignments to give people broader experiences. Someone might say, "I don't want to work on that audit another year or work with that partner, but in the model traditional firms follow, continuity is important to efficiency, competitive pricing, and profitability, so it is easier to keep people where they are at." The problem, of course, is that top performers will chafe at this and look elsewhere.

Getting partners to recognize the benefit of change is a challenge, especially when most are in their fifties or sixties with unfunded pension plans based on the last five years of practice, Siegfried says. "They are going to be asking, 'What will this do to my compensation?', and new or innovative ideas don't tend to get a lot of attention. And, when ideas come from younger people in their thirties or forties, they get shot down."

But you have to listen to what the market is telling you, Siegfried says. "I got into ARS just by answering the phone when DuPont called, and I figured there might be a business there. To me, collaborating is about listening to the client and finding out what is on their mind. For example, say you are doing the taxes, and the client's never paid more than $100,000. But his S-corp is booming, and now he owes about $1 million. What CPAs tend to focus on is, 'Did I calculate this right? Sure enough, the amount is $1,528,342.78.' But the client's real issue is, 'How are we going to pay for this?' Collaborating is about listening to the client and anticipating what is going to happen, not just sending over the file."

Collaboration with Clients Yields a Competitive Edge

When the IRS completely revamped Form 990, that changed a twelve-page document into an eighty-page one. The service dramatically expanded the scope from accounting-based reporting to activity-based reporting, according to CPA Geralyn Hurd, tax partner in Crowe Horwath LLP's Chicago office.

Geralyn Hurd, CPA,
tax partner
Crowe Horwath LLP
www.crowehorwath.com
Chicago, Illinois

"We saw the need to develop a software solution that would help tax-exempt organizations capture all the additional information required, while making it easy for those who are not tax people to understand what's needed and get good, accurate information without a lot of back and forth," Hurd says.

The result: Crowe Tax Risk Assessment and Control (C-TRAC®) a web-based, user-friendly, and IRS-approved software solution launched in 2008 and now used by hundreds of tax-exempt organizations nationally. "Like TurboTax it is wizard based, and depending on how you respond, it will take you to the next set of questions or requirements," Hurd says. "You don't need to know where the data will appear on the Form 990, and all the questions are user-friendly with explanations available if you need them."

Collaboration with clients began when she started to develop the product, and it has continued to this day—Version 5 was released in March 2013. Just one example is an add-on Alternative Investment Module, which addresses the needs of higher education institutions and private foundations, who are heavily invested in alternative investments. "They may have hundreds of millions in partnerships or foreign funds and receive anywhere from one hundred to four hundred Schedule K-1s for individual partnerships," she says. At year end they get a K-1 plus thirty to forty pages of whitepaper statements.

"That is a reporting nightmare for large institutions, who have full-time people doing nothing but aggregating the data and trying to handle international disclosures," she says. "You might have one K-1 that requires ten different international disclosures, and if you get it wrong, you are facing penalties of ten thousand dollars per form."

Crowe was first into the market with a software solution and still has commanding lead.

"C-TRAC has put us on the map," Hurd says. "Our practice has grown twenty-five percent per year, even in a tough economy. We have been able to focus strategically on large tax-exempt entities, and without this technology they would not have talked to us."

Her advice to other firms: "Get your clients to the table, and hear what they have to say before you pick up a pencil. Obviously you want to do some planning, but the earlier you can bring your customers and other skill sets together, the more likely you will succeed."

What about the naysayers? "The pushback I got from colleagues at other firms was, 'Why are you giving your client a lot of tools they can use to replace you as their tax preparer?' But my peers may have misunderstood the market," says Hurd. "If you give your client tools that will help them be successful, you are not minimizing your value, you are adding to it, because you have their best interest in mind."

Collaborative Selling: The Secret Sauce

This might be a good point to introduce a concept I hinted at in the opening scenario for this chapter. Once upon a time, a personal connection with a decision maker during a round of golf or over a drink on the nineteenth hole would result in a new client for the firm.

Sure, that can still happen, but it's becoming rare—especially in complex engagements involving serious money. It's far more likely you'll need to involve more than one person in the sales process (oh, I keep forgetting that the more palatable term in our industry is "business development," but who is kidding whom?).

The reasons are many, ranging from tighter corporate governance to jitters over the economy. But the net effect is the same: everyone from the board of directors on down is more risk averse.

In that kind of setting, structured buying processes on the client side coupled with a team approach minimize the risk of error. But rather than see these as frustrating roadblocks, top rainmakers are turning them into powerful competitive advantages.

Team with the Client

Advocate a collaborative, cross-functional team approach from the get-go, and it will play directly into the risk aversion that comes with changing "the way we've always done things around here." It also follows logically from your effort to improve collaboration within your firm: team members will be more comfortable with the idea.

In a collaborative process, you build a team consisting of your own client-facing people and those on the client side who will be responsible for implementing the solutions you provide. Bringing a group together like that as a team lets you control the conversation and more effectively tailor your solution. Among the benefits:

- **Broader buy-in.** Answers to questions arrived at together are much more compelling.

- **Deeper relationships.** Working together on a problem foreshadows how your organizations will partner together on future issues that emerge. That foreshadowing also builds a sense of relationship and trust that is essential to success.

- **Faster implementation.** This will allow for a quicker payoff for the client, since more key players "own" your solution.

How to Make It Happen

Think in terms of organizing collaborative events that bring the team together, whether it's around a conference table or via a remote videoconference. Here's where to start:

- **Have the outcome in mind.** You may want to explore a troubling problem the client faces. Perhaps you need to complete a needs analysis or diagram a business process before you present a solution. Either way, you need a clearly defined purpose for a meeting.

- **Make sure the right people are present.** Identify who needs to be on the team for maximum buy-in. Keep the number manageable. Six or seven people is optimal for collaboration.

- **Have a methodology for inviting people.** Prepare them in advance, and confirm they are going to be attending. E-mailing a confirmation is a good approach.

- **Prepare to host and facilitate.** During the event, you want to manage the agenda, promote interaction and transition from one topic to another.

- **Have an end point.** Given everyone's short attention span, plan on thirty-five- to forty-five-minute sessions. Distribute documentation to participants, and then follow up.

How to Increase Impact

To get people to attend, you need more than talking points. People will need to know what the result will be. It could be a decision, a choice to be made, a document, or a road map.

One person talking while others listen is instruction, not collaboration. To boost participation:

- **Ask people to play different roles.** Joe might serve as devil's advocate, while Sam takes the role of CEO. Key point: you come back to them in that role throughout the event.

- **Call on people to respond.** "Sue, how would that play out for you?" or "Bill, can you summarize what we just covered?"

- **Manage the clock.** You may need to table further discussion of a topic to keep things moving. The pace needs to be fast and on point.

- **Be sure to lock down outcomes.** Who is going to do what as a result of this meeting? Are we confident we have all the information we need? What are the action items?

If you are using GoToMeeting or another remote online venue, record the event and distribute a link to it. If questions arise from those who did not attend the meeting, attendees can be more effective at explaining what went on as well as the conclusions the group reached.

Visit Your Best Clients First

Chances are, this is a new way to approach the business development process, and like anything new, it will take practice to get comfortable with.

A good place to start is to identify one or two existing clients where you already have a solid relationship. Pick those that have problems that have surfaced in the past but remain unaddressed. It's likely they'll be open to experimenting with an interactive and collaborative approach. And in no time you'll be on your way to bigger engagements.

Visit www.boomer.com/collaboration and download

Collaboration Tool #6

The Client Collaboration Interview

Chapter Seven: Collaborating with Competitors

"That's a gimme," laughed Tom Mitchum as Sam Jones lined up a six-inch putt on the eighteenth green at Tuckaway Country Club. Sam picked up his ball, and the two walked back toward Bill Templeton, who was the first to hole out.

"Time to head for the nineteenth hole, eh?" Bill said as the three followed a winding path toward the clubhouse.

"I hate to bring up business," Tom said over a pint of ale, "but we are missing out on some serious opportunities to add revenue."

"Well, Mister-All-Business-All-The-Time," said Bill with a grin, "I owe Sam five bucks now. We had a side bet on how long it would take you to bring up something about the practice."

"OK, OK, I get it," Tom said. "But this is serious. The economy is turning around, at least a little bit, and more of our clients and prospects are facing complex problems that I am not sure we have the internal capability to address."

"Oh, come on, Tom," countered Sam. "We've always been able to figure things out. I admit that it often takes more time than it should."

Bill chimed in. "Where are you going with this, Tom? What are you thinking?"

"There's a lot of opportunity with current clients when it comes to cost segregation studies, for example, and the whole area of international tax, both of which could generate a lot of revenue for us," Tom explained. "But it will take time and money to develop the skills we need in those areas—and by that time we'll lose out."

"Sounds like a chicken and egg problem to me," Sam said. "Why not just keep doing what we're doing and not take the risk?"

"What we've done to get where we are won't get us to the next level," Tom said. "We're working on changing the culture and becoming more collaborative internally and with clients, but there's another thing we need to do."

"And what would that be?" asked Bill.

"I think we can reach out to another CPA firm—maybe more than one—to get the skills and experience we need to serve our clients in these areas," Tom said. "With the Internet and all, they would not need to be in our area."

"Are you nuts!" said Sam. "You better not have any more of that fancy ale you're drinking. What's to prevent them from stealing our clients away from us!"

"I think if we are careful and put together the right kind of arrangement, it can be a win for everyone involved, especially our clients," Tom said. "I intend to pursue it, starting bright and early Monday morning."

■

Collaborating internally and with clients is going to be increasingly important to the long-term success of CPA firms. A better approach to value creation—for all parties involved—is at the heart of it. As mentioned earlier, even arch-competitors like BMW and Toyota have agreed to collaborate, despite serving the same luxury automobile market. The two will share costs on electric car battery research, and BMW will supply diesel engines to Toyota, beginning with the 2014 model year. For the first time in its history, Toyota will sell its innovative hybrid engines to BMW.

Another example of collaboration for the common good is the Innovation Value Institute (IVI), a consortium aimed at enhancing the value of information technology and building collaboration between IT and business units.

The core consortium includes oil and gas competitors Chevron and BP, competing consulting firms Boston Consulting Group and Ernst & Young, and software companies Microsoft and SAP. Northrop Grumman is also part of the core group, as is Intel.

Each company has agreed to share its intellectual property, and the partners are all getting more out of the collaboration than the IP that they're investing in. Through the consortium, the members are shifting their thinking and approach from "competitive advantage to collaborative advantage," according to Martin Curley, Intel's global director of IT innovation, who codirects the institute, now housed at the National University of Ireland, Maynooth.

Ralf Dreischmeier,
senior partner and managing
director
Boston Consulting Group
www.bcg.com
Boston, Massachusetts

Historically, consortiums often deliver little more than announce-ments and joint news releases, because of the lack of true collabo-ration. "Five to ten years ago, this would have been dead," says Ralf Dreischmeier, partner and managing director of the Boston Consulting Group. "People were much more protectionist, thinking only about their little environment." He says IVI is succeeding because of the pre-mium its members are putting on *trust, sharing, and innovation*.

Identify the Right Opportunities

It's important to step back and think differently about how your firm can keep growing and leveraging current and future opportunities. You will most likely need to challenge some of your existing strate-gies and procedures—and biases. But there are ways to grow and prosper that move beyond the traditional "rugged individual" ap-proach many professionals are accustomed to. Collaborating with other firms is a viable alternative, especially for firms without the internal resources or client base to justify acquiring or hiring the necessary expertise.

One firm that's successful at collaborating externally is Baldwin CPAs, whose home base is in Richmond, Kentucky. Baldwin primarily serves construction contractors, financial institutions, governmental work, not-for-profit organizations, and nursing homes. "We do a lot of peer review work, and we collaborate with other firms and serve as an external resource for them on A&A engagements," says Alan Long, CPA, the managing partner.

Alan Long, CPA,
managing partner
Baldwin CPAs
www.baldwincpas.com
Richmond, Kentucky

He shares an example: "We serve one firm as their audit partner. My partner, who has expertise in governmental and nonprofit work, reviews every engagement they have and may be involved in some of the audit planning as well." The other firm is responsible for the engagement, Alan says. "We come in at the tail end, review the work papers in detail, and come up with review points. It's up to the other firm to decide internally which review points they want to address and clear—we don't follow up on that."

Technology streamlines the process, because both firms use the same audit software. "They just upload a backup for us to review." A good thing, since the other firm is located three hours away by car. "It works the same as if we were sitting there with them," Alan says. "We've also gone down there to conduct CPE for them as well." The payoff, of course, is that Baldwin gets additional revenue, while the other firm benefits from high-level audit expertise without having to have a high-level audit partner on their staff.

Baldwin also collaborates with a law firm client that does estate planning. "We started working together on a joint client, and that led to additional business valuation work for their other clients," Alan says. "Now, some of their clients weren't happy with their CPAs, so that turned into even more business."

His advice to other firms: "Don't look at other firms as competition; look at them as allies. You don't need to worry about cutthroat competition. If you treat each other professionally and deal with other good-quality firms, that is not going to be a problem. Too many CPAs have a 'head in the sand' problem and don't get out from behind the desk enough. You need to get out in the community and find out who the good firms are."

Collaboration as a Growth Strategy

"At the accounting firm of Green Hasson Janks, we believe that great things happen when people collaborate. For more than 55 years, it's been our privilege to work with individuals and organizations whose genius and audacity have shaped both the history and the future of Los Angeles."

That snippet from the GH&J website is only a hint of what the Los Angeles-based firm has been up to. As part of a rebranding effort in 2012, the word that kept floating to the surface in meeting after meeting was "collaboration." So that became the key brand promise: "Collaboration is the foundation for success," says Kari Schott, director of marketing, who served on the strategic planning committee at the firm.

Kari Schott,
director of marketing
Green Hasson Janks
www.greenhassonjanks.com
Los Angeles, California

With the help of consultant Jennifer Wilson of Convergence Coaching, the firm developed a 2016 Vision Initiative, mapping out where the firm plans to be in the next few years, with internal collaboration across the firm, not just partners and principals. "There's definitely excitement around this initiative," Schott says. "People are talking about it and coming to me with ideas. When I started three years ago, the traffic to my door was significantly less."

One quick win is that the firm has committed to growing industry niches, with food and beverage as a good example. "We started with one partner who had a passion for that market and saw the opportunity there," Schott says. "He'd pursued it independently with some success, but when we committed to it as a firm, the number of people involved grew, and a collaborative planning committee evolved."

The payoff: Schott says that overall firm growth in terms of clients and revenue is above industry averages. "In the double digits," she says. "And in the fifteen percent range for the food and beverage practice."

Collaborative opportunities have developed around special services for divorced individuals as well. "A tax partner and local CFP are working together to identify high-net-worth individuals who are forced to find new service providers because of the potential for conflict of interest issues or the desire to work with someone fresh," she says. The two are actively seeking law firms and developing a cosponsored, collaborative seminar event.

"Another way we promote collaboration is that we hold events specifically for service providers, with no clients or potential clients invited," Schott says. "We focus on areas where we all have common interests." Invitation-only mixers target specialists in mergers and acquisitions, food and beverage, and high-net-worth individuals. "We have a lot of people who thank us and say things like, 'That deal only got done because you made the introduction.'"

Collaborating on Training

Linda Steele founded Great Minds LLC a couple years ago at the behest of two Missouri firms who could not individually afford a full-time trainer but figured that they could share the costs. Together with Steele, they formed a joint venture to market her services to other small and midsize firms in the same boat.

"Now I work one week a month in Springfield, Missouri, for AbacusCPAs, another week in Sedalia, Missouri, for Wilson, Toellner & Associates LLC, and one week a quarter for Baldwin CPAs in Richmond, Kentucky," she says.

"Some smaller firms want a trainer once a quarter for a week, others one week a month," she says. They are geographically dispersed, so they don't compete directly with each other. "The firm in Sedalia serves mostly farmers and cattle ranchers, while the firm in Springfield has entertainment clients, since it's close to Branson."

Steele's training curriculum runs the gamut from soft skills to software. Subjects range from building effective teams to business body language and e-mail etiquette. "I've done a lot of client training as well, on things like QuickBooks, Outlook, and Office 2010. The firm can charge for that or not, as they see fit, to recover part of the cost of having me there."

Collaborating in Communities

As we've emphasized, collaboration to enable firm growth can take many forms. One approach is to join a community of peers that can accelerate your ability to balance opportunities with capabilities.

Boomer Consulting, Inc. can speak to this approach with over ten years of experience in facilitating communities. We started with The Boomer Technology Circles™ and then expanded to The CIO Advantage™, The Producer Circle™, The CEO Advantage™, and The Talent Development Advantage™.

We introduced you to Greg Davis, of Kennedy & Coe, in chapter six. As the firm's resident IT guru, he has participated in The Boomer

Technology Circles™ for several years. Some time ago, when no "off-the-shelf" software quite fit the bill, he wrote an in-house employee scheduling application to help the eight-office firm manage client projects, quickly see who was available, and match projects to staff.

Through The Boomer Technology Circles™, other firms found out about Davis's solution and, soon after, three other firms were using his brainchild in their firms. Another way the community has helped touches on the need for an objective outside viewpoint. "We have a technology committee that manages technology in our firm, and one benefit of the Circle is that we have added a CIO from another firm to our board so we get an outside firm perspective," Davis says.

Davis shares another quick payoff from The Boomer Technology Circles™: "When we were getting ready to implement a solution for secure mobile device management, we posted a question online and got input from many firms as to what they were using and happy with.

"That allowed us to more quickly come up with a solution and implement it. We had access to a half dozen firms that had already gone through implementation and could call on them for help. On the research side, that saved us fifty percent of the time and about twenty-five percent on implementation."

Visit www.boomer.com/collaboration and download

Collaboration Tool #7

The Competitor Strategy Action Plan

Chapter Eight: Encouraging Collaboration

"Well, pretty soon it's going to be that time of year again," said Managing Partner Tom Mitchum as he sank into the big chair in the paneled conference room at Mitchum, Jones & Templeton LLC. "Time to take stock of where we are at and decide who gets what in the way of salary and bonus."

Sam Jones weighed in. "Well, compensation seems pretty straightforward to me. Whoever bills the most time should get the most bucks."

"I don't know about that," said Bill Templeton. "Seems to me that I brought in a chunk of new business this year, but my billable hours were down. There ought to be a way that the lifetime value of that business gets taken into account."

"There's something else to consider," Tom said. "You know we've gone a long way toward changing the culture and becoming more collaborative. The team that went with you to that construction client and saved them fifty thousand dollars comes to mind. We need a way to encourage that kind of thing."

"Well, maybe we can give those two a bigger bonus, but to my way of thinking, it's all about the book of business and billable hours," Sam said. "The rest of it is touchy-feely human resources fluff. The way I was raised,

it's up to you to get ahead in this world. You work hard, you get rewarded, and that's that."

"Sam, I understand where you are coming from," Tom said. "But times are changing, and we've made a conscious effort to change the culture here to reflect that. I think the way we reward people needs to change as well. We want people to focus on clients, and we have to think about the good of the firm, and there's more to it than competing to see who can log the most billable time."

Bill Templeton spoke up. "We've had a good year, and a lot of that is because of people stepping up and doing more than they were asked to do. So I am OK with increasing the bonus pool. We've always allocated twenty percent of the firm profit to bonuses. Maybe it should go to thirty percent this time."

"I can go along with that idea," Sam said. "Just so long as we don't give people the idea that bonuses are always going to be that high."

The managing partner cleared his throat. "I want to take it a step further. This year let's put together a team of managers and senior staff to come up with bonus criteria and recommend how that thirty percent gets divided up. We'll make the final decision, of course, as owners. That will help promote the team approach we want to develop."

Bill's eyes lit up. You could tell he was on board. "And the criteria they use can go beyond just financials, huh? Rewards for learning and training? Or fresh ideas about policies and procedures? Or improved client service?"

"I don't know about this," Sam said. His body language spoke volumes. "How are you going to measure things like that? These changes you guys are making give me the willies!"

"Having a team come up with bonus criteria is a good start," Tom replied. *"What I really think we need to do is think more deeply about the behaviors we want to encourage and reward, like collaboration and being a team player. In the past we've used compensation to reward for building our book of business and billable hours, but it's just not that simple anymore."*

■

Linking Collaboration to Compensation

If you've had the same kind of conversations behind closed doors at your firm, you are not alone. In my experience, one of the biggest problems firms face today is that they put the compensation model together before they think about what they are trying to reward. When it comes to building a compensation model, many firms think in terms of job descriptions and salary banding. That is a good place to start—after all, you need a clear picture of skills and job duties for people at each level in the firm, and you want to make sure that salaries are at least competitive.

But there is more to it than that, especially when you are talking about building a collaborative, team-based culture, where you reward people for having great ideas, collaborating with others, and using their unique abilities to the fullest as part of a team approach to client service.

At Boomer Consulting, Inc. we see the Balanced Scorecard (BSC) approach as a much better way to translate strategy into action and to drive behavior change from the top down. It can work for firms of any size, and it focuses on four basic areas:

- learning and growth

- processes

- client satisfaction

- financial measures

Most firms have a handle on the financial measurements and focus the majority of their resources toward meeting financial goals. Metrics used as key performance indicators include revenue, charge hours, and net income before partners' salaries. Is this enough? In today's environment, the answer is no. It's like trying to fly an airplane while only monitoring airspeed.

Firms like the mythical Mitchum, Jones & Templeton that are working on changing their culture, improving their processes, training people, and promoting learning need broader measurements. And as we see in the example opening this chapter, this does not come without resistance in most firms.

The BSC approach involves developing overall strategic goals for the firm in the four categories mentioned above, then driving those goals down to the department level, and from there down to the individual. For example, each individual would be pushed toward setting goals that will allow the firm to be more collaborative and not just "me" oriented or one-sided.

Measuring Collaborative Behaviors

The metrics used in the BSC approach are broader. In the financial area, you can look at revenue per full-time equivalent, not just charge hours. You might also look at new clients or expanded service to existing ones. A lot of firms measure the lifetime value of a client, so a team that increases the lifetime value would be rewarded.

In the learning and training area, firms should be rewarding people for teaching and mentoring. A manager might be rewarded for learning new skills. A staff person might be rewarded for learning more on the technical side or maybe adding soft skills. It will be different for each individual, but the reward comes from accomplishing very specific goals within the learning and training area.

As a key point, learning should be measured by accomplishments rather than by the number of hours spent in the classroom. Learning only occurs efficiently when everyone has a personal learning plan and is rewarded for mastering the learning objectives. Those who don't accomplish their learning plans must be penalized through reduced compensation. There must be a penalty as well as a reward.

When considering the measurements for processes, you may want to have a category for following policies and procedures and another for improving policies and procedures. One example that comes to mind is streamlining tax return processing by eliminating bottlenecks or implementing new technologies like scanning or a client portal for paperless return delivery. A team that looks at each step in the process and finds ways to save time ought to be rewarded for that, even though not a single hour involved was billable.

On the client service side, firms are finding that client satisfaction surveys are fundamental (but again, nonbillable). Are they satisfied? Are we meeting their needs? Are people taking care of clients? Are they talking to clients? If collaboration is where the firm is going, has the firm dedicated a certain number of partner hours to visiting with clients "off the clock," as we described earlier? Or are partners sitting at their desk and logging billable time, just to gain bragging rights?

Let's look at sample Balanced Scorecards for an accounting firm, a partner, and a staff member. Note that the firm's strategic initiatives drive down to personal objectives. For best results, start with the firm and partners, then move down to managers and staff. The sample also shows the weight to give each initiative; however, each of the four sections gets equal points (25) on a scale of 100. The supervisor enters the score and creates the value. Consistency is important, so one person should manage the overall process.

Sample Firm Balanced Scorecard					
Perspective	Objectives	Weight	Points (Equal)	Score 1–10	Value
Financial	Increase revenue by 15%	10%	8.33		
	Increase revenue per FTE to $130k	5%	8.33		
	Increase net income before partners' salaries to 35%	10%	8.33		
Client satisfaction	Complete satisfaction surveys on 1/3 of clients	5%	8.33		
	Complete dangers, opportunities, and strengths worksheet on top 100 clients	15%	8.33		
	Terminate bottom 5% of clients	5%	8.33		
Internal processes	Define unique processes in tax preparation	5%	8.33		
	Implement document management system	10%	8.33		
	Outsource 250 tax returns to India	10%	8.33		
Employee Learning and Growth	Develop a training curriculum for each employee	5%	8.33		
	Hire a learning coordinator	10%	8.33		
	Provide a training facility	10%	8.33		
	Firm totals	100%	100.00		

Sample Partner Balanced Scorecard					
Perspective	Objectives	Weight	Points (Equal)	Score 1–10	Value
Financial	Increase managed book to $1,000,000	10%	8.33		
	Implement change orders in excess of $100,000	5%	8.33		
	Manage head count to $130k per FTE	10%	8.33		
Client satisfaction	Complete satisfaction surveys on 20 clients	5%	8.33		
	Complete dangers, opportunities, and strengths worksheet on top 20 clients	15%	8.33		
	Terminate bottom 5% of clients	5%	8.33		
Internal processes	Serve on technology committee	5%	8.33		
	Implement document management system	10%	8.33		
	Identify and outsource 75 1040 tax returns	10%	8.33		
Employee Learning and Growth	Attend 40 hours of internal training	5%	8.33		
	Complete securities licensing	10%	8.33		
	Develop advanced financial reporting class with learning coordinator	10%	8.33		
	Firm totals	100%	100.00		

	Sample Staff Balanced Scorecard				
Perspective	**Objectives**	**Weight**	**Points (Equal)**	**Score 1–10**	**Value**
Financial	Increase production to $175,000	10%	8.33		
	Identify change orders in excess of $10,000	5%	8.33		
	Target 5 new clients of greater than $5,000 each	10%	8.33		
Client satisfaction	Complete satisfaction surveys on 5 clients	5%	8.33		
	Complete dangers, opportunities, and strengths worksheet on top 5 clients	15%	8.33		
	Identify 3 "underperforming" clients	5%	8.33		
Internal processes	Serve on tax processing task force	5%	8.33		
	Convert client files to new FR system	10%	8.33		
	Identify 20 returns for outsourcing	10%	8.33		
Employee Learning and Growth	Attend 40 hours of internal training	5%	8.33		
	Complete MOUS certification	10%	8.33		
	Obtain CITP designation	10%	8.33		
	Firm totals	100%	100.00		

Note that the sample scorecards show consistency, accountability, and measurable goals. You should also realize this will require management time and commitment in order for it to be successful. Don't be surprised if people resist. The concept promotes meritocracy rather than mediocrity. As mentioned, start small (firm and partners) and then progress to the point where you include the staff in the process. Quarterly reviews of progress are also advised.

Firms who have implemented the Balanced Scorecard say it is about progress and not perfection. It drives behavior based upon the firm's strategic plan to the partners and then on to managers and staff. This requires good communication and time to manage—technical skills are not the only requirement for a winning team. When the behaviors are focused on collaboration, the Balanced Scorecard can help build a collaborative environment with measurable results.

Winning teams need coaches whose primary concern is to provide the necessary resources to managers and staff and maintain their confidence. Too many partners spend the majority of their time working *in* the business rather than *on* the business. The BSC approach gives partners a way to help others succeed and gain leverage.

Performance Management

The Balanced Scorecard approach makes it easier to manage performance from top to bottom in a CPA firm, because it incorporates results-based **planning** and gives managers (coaches) the opportunity to give **regular feedback**, not only quarterly but in the moment. The opportunity to **evaluate** performance based on statistics, observations, and other data is built-in as well.

People need consistent, real-time feedback to accelerate their learning and improve their performance. In fact, lack of feedback is one of the most common complaints we hear from staff at firms we've worked with. For example, at one firm, we asked people what one thing they would change, and almost all said they did not feel like a family anymore. It was "come to work, do your job, go home."

This was disappointing to hear because people inherently want to do a good job. Your people don't come to work in the morning with aspirations of being average or mediocre, unless they are so discouraged that they are just simply doing a job. People have a natural human desire to do well, perform, and improve. It is the way we are wired. In situations like these, it is essential to examine the management and culture of the firm because this is where the work environment is generated and propagated. The first step to resolving this disconnect is to increase (or incorporate) feedback.

Delivering feedback is a skill that too many managers and partners do not possess, and therefore they either avoid giving effective feedback or give it in ways that are not helpful. Most people can learn how to deliver feedback effectively, meaning that it is given truthfully, in a way it can be heard and acted upon. Feedback without one or more of these characteristics isn't helpful and can be hurtful. Because most people have experienced receiving feedback in unhelpful or hurtful ways, it is no wonder they resist giving it when they become managers and partners.

Performance feedback comes in two forms: confirming and corrective. Confirming feedback reinforces behavior by identifying what people are doing right and recognizing their effort, actions, and results. If you tell a staff person you appreciate the way they submit their work to you, they are most likely to submit it in the future the same way. The management principle is this: what gets recognized gets repeated. Most of the time, we only look for what is not right and notice it, at the exclusion of confirming feedback. When people do what they are supposed to do, why say something about it? If you want people to continue to behave in certain ways, recognize it.

Corrective feedback is used when behavior is expected to be changed, modified, or improved. This can be a very powerful management tool as long as it is delivered effectively. By focusing on the behavior, linking it to career development and firm goals, and stating it in a respectful, supportive tone, people are motivated to change and adapt.

For best results, hold managers and partners accountable to learn how to give effective feedback, build it in their development plans, track and monitor their feedback effectiveness, and reward their efforts and results, and you will soon have a firm that accelerates performance.

(For complete details, including checklists you can use to evaluate your current performance management system, see "The Guide to Performance Management," available at www.boomer.com.)

Relaxation Leads to Motivation

You have to take time to relax and breathe in order to keep people motivated and excited about what the firm is doing. In an earlier chapter, we spoke about the way WithumSmith + Brown worked collaboratively to produce their wildly successful viral videos. The real key to success was letting more people get involved and join in the fun. That's true whether you are investing time in developing a video or doing something much more modest.

Most firms will say that's what our COO does or our firm administrator is responsible for. But we think that the fun things firms do are more successful when the partners are involved and willing to "let their hair down." Here are some examples:

- At Raymon Pielech Zexter (now part of LarsonAllen LLP), the firm installed a Wii system and ran an electronic bowling league, with teams of partners versus staff, complete with prizes and trophies. "The younger staff were far more proficient at it," CPA Robert Pielech admitted.

Robert Pielech, CPA
LarsonAllen LLP
www.larsonallen.com

- At Houston-based Weaver LLP, tax partner Samuel F. Wren, CPA, reported that his firm cuts the tax season tension by taking off to have partner versus staff paintball matches. "It's a great way to build teamwork and relieve stress, but you can have sore muscles the next day," he says. "Those paintballs can hurt."

Samuel F. Wren, CPA,
tax partner
Weaver LLP
www.weaverllp.com

- Adams, Brown, Beran and Ball, a multi-office firm headquartered in Great Bend, Kansas, conducts an electronic bingo game during tax season that's a great motivator. It's conducted over the network, takes very little time out of the day, and is well received because people win prizes ranging from dinner for two to an iPod or DVD player.

- HeimLantz, an Annapolis, Maryland, business accounting and consulting firm, has a tradition of doing something different every Wednesday afternoon, just to make sure everyone is having fun. Examples range from spending the afternoon bowling or shooting pool to going to the movies.

Motivation doesn't have to cost much or be elaborate. The managing partner at a firm in Minneapolis dons a big white chef's hat and cooks breakfast for everyone. He brings in his griddle and makes pancakes for everybody. They look forward to it and talk about it. When I surveyed the staff and asked what they liked most, everyone said, "When our managing partner cooks us breakfast." Another firm sets up hallway bowling. The managing partner put it this way: "Every once in a while, when I feel the stress is too high, I will set it up in the hallway for five or ten minutes or so and gather people together to roll a line or two."

The real key to success is that things like this need to be: (1) sporadic, not planned, and (2) a partner doing it. That way it feels real and genuine, not forced or fake, like an item from your checklist. That is what makes it real and motivational.

Some of these events take place during busy season, but firms are looking at other times of the year as well. For example, they let people work Monday through Thursday and close on Fridays during the summer. One firm does something that's even more motivating: they let people pick the day they want to take off.

They tell staff, "We are open five days a week, but we want you to pick a day that you don't want to be here." The firm assumed everyone would pick either Monday or Friday, but several picked Tuesday, Wednesday, or Thursday. Why? The kids were busy in school, and those were the best days to go to the grocery store or run errands because no one else was out. The good thing about this was it allowed people to figure out their own work/life balance.

The Last Piece of the Puzzle: Compensation

Let's say you have put together a Balanced Scorecard that drives the collaborative behaviors you want, you have put a performance management system in place that gives people the feedback they need, and you have taken steps to build a fun atmosphere.

What's next? You need a compensation model that will reward those behaviors, and it is the last piece of the puzzle. Look at what you are doing now in terms of compensation, and ask yourself if it is rewarding the behaviors you want. What good does it do if you to go through all this and at the end of the year, when it's time to make decisions about compensation, you go back to looking at billable time?

If that's all you look at, your people will figure out in a New York minute that nothing else really matters. And as a result, people will focus on billable time like they always have, and the rest of what you want to accomplish for the firm will fall by the wayside.

The exclamation point is compensation, and everyone needs to be on the same page. It will fall apart if you have one or two people who are not on board, who don't really believe, and only pretend to drink the Kool-Aid. An "all about me" type of person, regardless of age or position, is not going to work in a collaborative setting and may even sabotage what you are trying to do. It's all about shared vision, not shared services, and those people who get that, who realize that we are much more amazing together than we are apart, are those who will succeed and prosper.

Visit www.boomer.com/collaboration and download

Collaboration Tool #8

The Balanced Performance Approach

Chapter Nine: Eliminating Not-So-Hidden Barriers to Collaboration

Tom Mitchum was taking a long time adding the half-and-half to his coffee mug and took extra time stirring with his spoon. He was buying time, not knowing quite how to proceed. Finally he looked across the desk at his partner, Sam Jones.

"Sam, I don't want to pussyfoot around. Let me just get it out on the table so we can discuss it. I get the feeling you are not buying in to the direction we want to take the firm. Is that a fair statement?"

"I have been trying to adjust to the changes you want to make," Sam said. "But it is really tough for me. I am probably too old and set in my ways at this point."

"As I've said before, Sam, doing a better job of what we've always done isn't enough anymore. We need to make these changes in order to keep from losing clients and talented young people. The future of the firm depends on it."

Sam shrugged. "I hear what you are saying, and some of what we've done, like staying in closer touch with clients, makes good sense. But I really don't like the idea of dropping timesheets. How are we going to keep people accountable for their time? How are we going to know if we are making a profit? And this business of letting staff work from home rubs me the wrong way, too. They are going to be watching soap operas instead of billing time, I just know it."

Tom smiled. "Well, nobody watches soaps anymore, Sam. And with the technology we have nowadays, people can work from anywhere. I think we have to give our young staff more flexibility and trust them."

Sam's body language spoke volumes. "Tom, let me be candid. I am a couple years from retirement, and as you know, our compensation model rewards for building a book of business and logging billable time. A lot of what you are asking of me—working with younger people, collaborating, and all that—involves sacrificing billable hours. I'm just not comfortable with that."

Tom nodded. "I get that, I really do. That's why we need to rework our compensation as part of the change in culture. That way you won't get penalized. I don't want to be in a situation like they faced at Marshall & Co., where the retiring managing partner did everything he could to maximize book of business. He cut expenses to the bone, essentially raping the firm, in order to maximize his own payout, which was based on profitability over the final two years."

Sam leaned forward. "I'll be interested in seeing how that plays out. Just remember how much my book of business has meant to the firm."

■

The Northbound Train Effect

In *The Northbound Train*, his 1994 book on linking strategic direction to customer value, consultant and business visionary Karl Albrecht said, "You must have a vision for your success and a direction for getting there. You have to know what train you are going to ride." In addition to setting defined goals, you need determined and empowered employees powering the engine. Of course, all the thinking and planning involved is for naught if the people in your firm are not on board.

As a profession, we tend to hire quickly and fire slowly. Long-established traditions in practice place a premium on technical skill sets and loyalty. Plus, many firms take pride in having developed a family environment. After all, who wants to fire a member of the family?

For a collaborative culture to take effect, you have to be willing to let go of people. If you have someone who truly cannot get aboard, then counsel them to change, or counsel them out. That is a hard thing to do, but it is imperative. You simply cannot get a collaborative environment to work if there are people who do not support it and want to keep things as they were. Doing so will sabotage all your effort.

As we have said earlier, the move toward a collaborative culture starts at the top of the organization, so it is particularly important for the firm's leadership to be in synch. One of the most effective ways to ensure that owners and managers are on the same page is to conduct a 360-Degree Evaluation of the leadership group. The focus should be specifically on leadership skills and how they engage with their team.

Traditionally, 360-degree appraisals have four components:

1. **Self-appraisal** lets the employee look at his/her strengths and weaknesses, his achievements, and judge his own performance.

2. **Superior appraisal** forms the traditional part of the 360-degree performance appraisal, where the boss rates the employee's responsibilities and actual performance.

3. **Subordinate appraisal** judges the employee on parameters like communication and motivating abilities, the ability to delegate the work, and leadership qualities.

4. **Peer feedback** can help assess an employee's ability to work in a team as well as co-operation and sensitivity toward others.

Self-assessment is an indispensable part of 360-degree appraisals and can be a real eye-opener, with high impact on behavior and performance. When conducted at regular intervals (say, yearly), 360s help track behavior changes as well as others' perceptions, which can be equally revealing.

I recently worked with a four-partner firm where the partners were not acting like nice people and faced a real problem with favoritism. Each partner had his own favorites on the staff, but they didn't think it was obvious. "I feel closer to so-and-so," one of them told me, "but no one sees that." Except that when we conducted a 360-Degree Evaluation in their firm, everyone saw the favoritism and commented on it, and they hated it.

Conducting a 360-Degree Evaluation is a huge commitment, but it can be extremely rewarding. It's very difficult to do with people who know each other, and we recommend bringing in an outside person who has the training and experience needed to help firm leaders understand what behaviors must change and will hold them accountable.

Competition for Dad's Attention

The second hidden barrier to building a collaborative environment is the idea of competing for attention. That can be a problem because in a collaborative environment, we are all equals, and it doesn't matter what your title is or what you are paid.

The reality is we are all valuable, and together we make a difference. When someone in your midst needs all the attention, has all the answers, and doesn't value what others have to say or contribute, they are not going to be a good team player.

One real-world example comes from Lawhorn CPA Group Inc. in Knoxville, Tennessee. We introduced Jason Lawhorn in an earlier chapter, describing how the firm adopted a collaborative, team approach to dramatically improve client service. In the process they did away with titles. "We don't think the hierarchy of junior, senior, and manager really works," Jason says. "So everyone's business card simply reads Team Professional."

Jason Lawhorn,
managing partner
Lawhorn CPA Group Inc.
www.lawhorncpa.com
Knoxville, Tennessee

Not everyone bought into the change to a flatter, more collaborative approach, and the firm has a smaller staff now. "The ones who were looking for power and authority have gone, because they realized we are not going to operate that way anymore. People whose egos need structure aren't a good fit," says Lawhorn.

One way Lawhorn ensures that people remain committed is by conducting quarterly reviews. Jason explains: "They tell me what their achievements have been, and we talk about improvements. Then we talk about their frustrations and mental roadblocks and look for solutions: What is the strategy for moving past this? Then we realign focus for the next ninety days. This is not an official review about money but a way to communicate with them so they know I am listening."

My Timesheet Is Bigger Than Yours

Keeping track of time in fifteen-minute increments and billing by the hour is certainly the traditional way firms have operated. And in that kind of environment, whoever bills the most time or brings in the most business typically gets the highest rewards. The problem is that in a collaborative culture, tracking time by the hour puts everyone's emphasis on the time spent doing the work, not the value delivered to the client. The solution is to break with tradition and dump the timesheets in favor of value pricing.

One of many firms that have done so is TYS LLP in San Ramon, California. We introduced readers to this firm back in chapter two, illustrating its collaborative style and describing how the partners wanted to move away from the profession's two-hundred-year-old way of running a practice.

Glen Thomas, CPA, partner
TYS LLP
www.tysllp.com
San Ramon, California

"We believe that we will be better off having a collaborative environment as opposed to a hierarchical environment," Thomas says, and he has established a results-only operating environment, in which members of the firm do not track their time.

Thomas continues, "We sit with clients and determine the scope of services they will need for the year and create a Fixed Price Agreement, which often spreads out over twelve months. When we send invoices, they've already agreed to the amount, and we don't have that challenge to deal with. It smoothes out our cash flow and does the same for clients as well."

The traditionalist would say, How do you know you are making money? "Accountants should know how to figure out whether you are making a profit," Thomas says. "When it comes to specific client engagements, the idea of tracking time has some merit to it, and candidly it forces us to give feedback within our team to really understand whether we are getting the right price for it or not.

"There is no doubt one of the challenges is 'scope creep,' and I am sure that with this approach we lose opportunities for billings. But we think the advantages far outweigh the negatives, because of the positives we create with clients," Thomas says. "What we've found is that putting the focus on serving the client means I can go to anyone in my firm who can help—even another partner—without worrying about the impact on billings."

Of course, the issue of value pricing compared to tracking and billing by the hour continues to generate lively debate, and a comprehensive discussion of the topic is beyond the scope of this book. To dig deeper into the issues, consider visiting www.verasage.com, the website of Ron Baker's VeraSage Institute. Ron has written extensively on value-based pricing; his latest book is *Pricing on Purpose: Creating and Capturing Value*.

Who's Winning the Turf War?

Closely related to the "my timesheet is bigger" issue is the idea that "these are *my* clients. I brought them into the firm, they are *mine*, and I will control what happens to them and who gets access to them." Time and again we have seen clients jealously guarded this way, inhibiting cross-selling of other profitable firm services, as well as client service issues.

Such "turf wars" may come about as a result of the way firms are structured, with separate tax, audit, and consulting departments, each with a partner in charge and a Chinese wall separating them. It may also come about as a result of what we call a "shared services" approach to operating a practice, as opposed to a "shared vision" of the firm and the idea that everyone needs to be moving in the same direction.

In either case, you most likely will need an outside facilitator to help work through these issues and break down barriers to taking a collaborative approach.

Boomers versus Generations X and Y

Firms dominated by partners/owners from generations prior to X often continue to put in long hours, routinely place their job before personal priorities, have limited (if any) flexible work arrangements, and typically expect others to "toe the line" in order to get ahead.

There are two key ways this affects firms, and neither of them bode well for growth and success of a thriving practice:

- **Work/Life Balance.** Members of the firm, from partners to admin staff, often experience burnout, low productivity, dissatisfaction, and increased stress, largely due to a lack of balance between their work and personal lives. This is not an easy issue to address, since what looks like balance to one person may differ for another because individuals have different goals, values, and definitions of success.

  A good place to begin to understand the issue of work and life balance is with a common definition: (1) having a sense that there is enough time in the day to effectively accomplish work-related tasks; (2) the ability to get through our daily work and family responsibilities without feeling drained; and (3) having the ability to participate in activities we enjoy on a regular basis.

  Key point: The key to balance is all in your head. Begin to think differently! So many accountants feel guilty about focusing on work/

life balance, or they believe taking time out for themselves—away from work—is an unproductive use of time. I'll tell you what I tell my clients, GET OVER IT!

- **Collaboration Is the New Normal.** Those of us who are boomers made our way in the world by being individualists. Our parents said things like, "If you want something, you have to go out and work for it. There is no free lunch." They didn't say, "Find a group and participate." So collaboration is not normal for people leading firms today, and most firms are built on the premise that "it's about *you*, not about other people."

When it comes to collaboration, though, younger people have grown up with it. My daughter, now twenty-one, started working in small groups fifteen years ago in kindergarten. In fourth grade she was working with the same model of "pods" of people in the classroom. They would exchange papers and grade each other. The teacher was there to supervise and facilitate. That same experience carried forward through high school and college.

Key point: Younger professionals have grown up collaborating and will expect it when they enter your firm, just as they will expect to find leading edge technology and mobile apps (see chapter eleven for more on how technology enables collaboration).

The biggest issue is breaking old habits and understanding that the old way is not wrong, it's just that the new way is so much better. Younger people entering our profession now are betting that attitudes and opportunities will open up. Those from older generations need to capitalize on the opportunity as well, and appreciate how generations X and Y and millennials can contribute new thinking and innovative ideas that will make the firm more profitable—and life more enjoyable.

How Much is *This* Going to Cost?

One key factor affecting the move toward a collaborative culture is the cost, in terms of the time involved and the overall effect on the billable versus nonbillable time incurred. While it is going to require nonbillable time to implement all of this, that investment will come back to you in terms of higher client and staff retention as well as higher billings, especially if you trash the time card and switch to value pricing agreements and change orders correctly.

The strategy has paid off at TYS LLC, as Glen Thomas explains. "We sit together as a team and decide what our 'Big Rocks' for the year will be. For 2012, we created a Growth and Profitability Rock and allocated responsibility eighty-five percent to the owners and fifteen percent to nonowners. The target was set at fifteen percent growth, but because we made the goal tangible and specific for each individual, we closed the year at twenty percent in growth. Profitability is twice what we budgeted as well."

Another thing the firm does is split the profit pie in thirds. "We retain one-third for the firm, one-third goes to the partners, and one-third of the profit is shared by the nonowners," Thomas says. "That's different from the typical firm, which is more likely an eighty/twenty profit split. What's more, the nonowners recommend how their share is divvied up; shareholders make the final decision, but we usually only tweak those recommendations a bit," says Thomas.

The compensation model for partners can become a sticking point if it is not addressed directly as part of changing the culture of the firm. If it is set up to reward people for their personal book of business and billable time, it is going to affect the willingness of partners and managers to sacrifice the billable time needed to make these changes happen or to change their behavior. That can be a particular issue for partners who are approaching retirement, especially when buyout agreements are written based on the last two years of compensation.

A better approach: revise compensation models to reflect how the business is doing overall, how people are being trained and developed, and reward for efforts at collaboration. This gets back to working *in* your business, rather than *on* the business. It's easy to get so wrapped up in bringing in new business and being billable that you forget to work *on* the business itself.

Handling Difficult Conversations

I want to close this chapter by discussing one of the biggest hidden barriers to culture change and collaboration, which is simply the issue that people are often unwilling to open up and tell the real truth about what is going on. There are a number of reasons for this dynamic, ranging from a desire not to ruffle any feathers, to not wanting to cause trouble, to not wanting to open themselves up to criticism.

Here is a recent example: I worked with a four-partner firm that was on the verge of breaking apart, because each partner was angry about what the others were doing, and they had a lot of "baggage" they did not want to share.

In advance of my first visit, each partner called to let me know what was wrong with the other partners and to share what I needed to know before I came in to work with them. At the meeting I was to facilitate, I said, "Let's play a game: we'll go around the room, and each of you will say to the others, 'Here is something you should keep doing because you are spectacular at it. Here is something I believe you should do differently because it will help you be a better person. And here is something you should stop doing because it is driving me crazy or harming the firm.'"

I emphasized that this was not the time to hold back and that it was a safe environment in which they could tell the truth. But as the meeting progressed, not one of those partners said out loud the things they said to me about the other ones on the phone. I let them finish (it takes a couple of hours to do this right with four partners), and at the end they, all said things like, "This was great. I got to say things I really wanted to say."

I smiled and said, "I call bullshit! All of you called me to talk about what you were angry about or disappointed about or challenged with, and not one of those things you told me came up in the conversation we just had. Not one." They stopped. They laughed. They looked guilty. They knew they were caught. They had self-edited or dissembled, telling only part of the truth, not the full story.

I said, "I told you this was the time to tell the truth. So go back and do it again. This is the time and place to get it all out." They did that, and it was absolutely a turning point in their firm. Later they told me that during the day together they had the most powerful conversations they had ever had, and it changed the firm profoundly for the better.

Sessions like that can work out well, especially when you have a trained facilitator involved. Two books on the subject are well worth reading: *Crucial Conversations: Tools for Talking When the Stakes Are High* by Kerry Patterson, and *Fierce Conversations* by Susan Scott. Both provide tools and strategies you can use to bring up uncomfortable subjects or things that go unsaid in life, which happens a lot in close relationships like business partnerships and marriages.

Another particularly valuable technique comes from The Rainmaker Group, which conducts a Five Star session dealing with internal and external customers. One of the steps is called Ascertaining Satisfaction, which is very powerful. For leaders, it involves having a deeper conversation with coworkers than "How's it going?"

Ascertaining Satisfaction involves asking two questions (perhaps over lunch): "What am I doing that is valuable and you want me to keep doing?" and then "What am I doing today that I should change or stop doing that would make our relationship better?" However, the key is to make sure that you are putting yourself in a position to get the best feedback possible. This could be done by setting up an appointment in advance and letting the person know the two questions that you will be asking so he or she has time to thoughtfully consider his or her answers. It's a scary thing to ask because you don't know what he or she going to say, but nearly everyone who has been on the receiving end has found the advice on point and valuable. Of course you have to act on the advice to change your behavior.

We do this at Boomer Consulting, Inc., and what I heard was, "You have to stop working at night, because when you work at night, that makes everyone here feel like they should—and you should stop that." Another person said to me, "You need to treat yourself better and get more sleep—because it affects how you work and will affect the team." These are very good conversations that we probably would never have had otherwise. Plus, it makes us a far more collaborative, close-knit group of people.

You have to have real trust with the people you are sitting across from. You have to go to them with no ill will, no matter what they say, and thank them. You may not agree with it, but you need to understand that they are giving you *their truth*. This is a great way to eliminate barriers, but you have to make sure that you don't look at them and say something like, "Are you kidding? I don't do that!"

The Ascertaining Satisfaction conversation helps you have conversations in a proactive and positive way. Some people assume that tough conversations have to be negative. But I don't believe that. It can be extremely positive if done the right way, in a safe environment.

How do you create a safe environment? That comes from leadership and involves building a culture in which everyone has a voice and everyone feels safe to say what they think. That doesn't mean that everyone will always agree, but it does mean that you are safe to say what you think and have a conversation about it, without having it escalate into anger.

Understanding other people's personalities and work style will help when you have those kind of conversations. Chances are, as a leader, if you go to someone else to try to change them, it probably won't work. But if you ask, "What could I do to get better?" you have given them permission to open up. And when you do that, they are more likely to do the same for you. When a person in leadership admits he or she doesn't know everything and is willing to change, that willingness to be vulnerable makes a huge difference.

■

In this chapter we've covered the need to get everyone "on board" when it comes to building a collaborative environment and how to deal with the not-so-hidden barriers involved. In the next chapter, you'll learn about a breakthrough approach in recruiting that ensures new people you add to the firm will bring the collaborative skills you need.

Visit www.boomer.com/collaboration and download

Collaboration Tool #9

Transforming Fear to Strength

Chapter Ten: Recruiting and Developing Future Collaborators

"Now that we've reviewed the numbers for the month, let's move on to the next item on the agenda," said Managing Partner Tom Mitchum, "future staffing needs."

"I need to find a couple of new people for the tax department," said Sam Jones.

"Two?" said Bill Templeton. "What is going on over there, Sam? I thought you only needed one new person to handle the increase in high-end 1040s."

"So did I," Sam replied, shifting in his seat. "But it turns out that Sally's husband is being transferred to North Carolina, and she is leaving at the end of the month. At least we are through the peak of busy season. Only a few returns are on extension this time around."

Tom leaned in. "Has she found a job down south?

"Not that I know of," said Sam. "In fact I think she might be expecting."

"Have you thought about keeping her on staff and letting her work remotely?" asked Tom. "I hate to lose someone with her creativity and skills."

"That's just not practical," Sam said. "Besides, it will cost too much."

Bill chimed in at this point. "I think we can just set her up with the same system she has now, dual monitors and all. We should at least try it and see how it works."

"I need someone here in the office," Sam argued. "The returns we handle are too complex. Maybe if we were talking about wage-earner returns it would be different. I just don't want to make mistakes with those high-income clients."

"The way I see it, there are two issues to resolve before we go much further," Tom said. "First, we need to explore how we can use technology to solve this problem, while making sure Sam's concerns are addressed. I think we can do both, actually. And the second thing is to think more deeply about what we should look for in a new hire."

"Well, in a perfect world, I'd like someone with a couple years of tax prep experience," Sam said. "But certainly someone who is detail oriented and technically savvy. After all, they will be under my direct supervision, for a while at least."

Tom coughed. "I see where you are coming from, Sam. But we need to hire someone who will fit with the collaborative culture we are moving toward. That is, someone who is a team player, who can think through problems on his or her own, who can communicate with clients, and who has people skills. I don't think that we should just hire a warm body to get the work out."

Sam bristled. "I think it's dangerous to let some young associate communicate with clients. I wouldn't let that happen for quite a while."

"Sam, you need to get used to the idea that anyone we hire is going to be intelligent and will resent being treated like a child. Nowadays, young staff are ready for more responsibility a lot sooner than we ever were."

■

In *Good to Great*, author Jim Collins explains the importance of "getting the right people on the bus" as the first step toward creating a vision for greatness. He stresses that your team should not be tied to a specific firm strategy because strategies will change over time. Instead your team should be committed to your firm and fit with your culture. In this chapter we'll dig deeper into applying this approach to your firm's hiring process so that you achieve peak performance and build a collaborative culture.

It makes a lot of sense to get this right, because hiring the wrong person typically costs three times their base salary when you add up all the hard and soft dollars involved in starting back at square one, according to research by the Society of Human Resource Management. Recruiting and training costs are obvious, but there's also lost productivity and a drain on the pool of intellectual capital.

The biggest problem we see is that CPA firms are too nice. Firms tend to hold on to people who don't live up to everyone's expectations. There are several possible reasons for this: the work needs to get done, and a "warm body" is better than nothing; hiring mistakes make everyone look bad; or everyone may just want to avoid conflict. No matter what the reason, the long-term effects are often more damaging than the short-term rewards.

Another issue is that leaders have a tendency to hire and promote people that are just like them. They have the same educational background, are similar in how they fit the culture, have a personality that matches and often even work the same way in details, vision, or organization.

The problem is that if there are lots of "clones" running around the firm, there will be pieces missing from the puzzle that you need to make a complete synergistic team. If you have a firm full of very detail-oriented team members, you may miss the vision needed to identify new opportunities; if the firm is full of visionaries, you may miss the processes that will lead to a productive firm that can do more with less. The great firms have diversity, and diversity comes with from intentional thought and planning when making hiring decisions.

Building a unique and collaborative team is not easy. Firms must begin thinking like they are putting together a puzzle. The pieces are all uniquely different, but if they are placed together with thought and care, your team will help create a clear picture of your firm's vision.

Develop and Use a Hiring Profile

It's far better to hire the best, mentor them, and motivate them to work to their highest capabilities. The first step to hiring and retaining team members who will be great contributors to your firm is to develop a detailed profile of the employee you wish to hire. This approach goes beyond the standard job description to an analysis of the personal attributes, strengths, and technical skills the new hire will need to be successful with your firm, such as curiosity, high energy, people skills, team orientation, and the ability to change. If you complete this step correctly, the odds of finding and keeping the right person are vastly improved.

As you develop the candidate profile, analyze your firm and your current culture. With this analysis as a foundation, build a list of personal attributes required for this new employee to be successful. When you are changing your culture so that it is less hierarchical and more collaborative, you will want to base the profile on what you want the culture to be. When interviewing candidates, be sure to explain this to them, and list attributes such as collaborative work style in your profile.

A strength, as defined by Marcus Buckingham and Donald Clifton in *Now, Discover Your Strengths*, is "consistent near perfect performance of an activity." In their book they document research supporting the premise that to achieve peak performance a person must be maximizing their strengths. If you can match a person's natural talent with how he or she spends most of his or her time on the job, he or she will reach his or her level of peak performance in your firm. In addition, he or she will be truly committed and fulfilled by his or her work. This gives you the added benefit of hiring a person who will not be easily enticed to leave your firm.

Most positions in CPA firms require a certain level of skills and specialized knowledge. This section of the profile should consider the time it takes to acquire specific skills as well as how long those skills will be relevant to the job. Most unsuccessful hires are a result of a mismatch of personal attributes or "chemistry," not a lack of technical skills. The best person for the position may be a candidate who has the personal attributes to succeed and lacks skills that can quickly be acquired. Be sure to include distinctions between required and desired attributes for the position.

Get Everyone's Expectations Right

In chapter five we introduced you to the Kolbe Index and how it can help find the right fit when hiring or creating collaborative teams. Testing for a good fit using the Kolbe Index will help you align the candidates' natural instincts with the expectations you have for the job you are trying to fill. You'll get a clearer picture of how well a person is likely to perform in the role and match the talent profile.

To review briefly: The Kolbe A™ Index is a thirty-six-question test that measures the "conative" or instinctive strengths that drive the way a person takes action—his or her "modus operandi," if you will. The Kolbe B™ Index measures how a person views the demands of his or her own position and the strengths that are a natural fit for the job. Kolbe C™ Index measures someone else's expectations for the specific position, such as a team leader, supervisor, or owner.

Analyzing the results of all three indexes has a high payoff in revealing an individual's strengths as well as the strengths of those they work with. It is particularly valuable when it comes to filling open positions, because different people will have different expectations for what is needed for a new hire to succeed.

In a recent example at Boomer Consulting, Inc. we had three firm leaders complete the Kolbe C™ Index for an open position in business development. That brought to light similarities and differences in expectations that were hashed out until we arrived at a strong consensus and understanding about the type of candidate we were looking for. Later, when candidates completed the Kolbe A™ Index, an online report for each candidate showed how they matched our expectations for the position.

The same concepts apply to building project teams. We use the Kolbe A™ Index results for each individual to help assemble teams most likely to be productive and get top-notch results. We've found that well-balanced teams need a blend of researchers, innovators, and process-oriented members, for example.

Another thing we do that helps to ensure we make the right hiring decisions is to have the top candidates meet everyone on the Boomer Consulting team in a group session. That way, everyone has a chance to ask questions and get a feeling for the candidate's fit with our culture. Afterward, there's a candid discussion of pros, cons, plusses, and minuses—followed by a yes/no vote.

While it may not be feasible for everyone in your firm to meet with potential new hires, try getting a cross-functional team involved. Include one representative from each department, and conduct at least one group interview session. You'll be surprised by the insight and broader perspective you'll gain through a collaborative hiring process.

Develop a Recruiting Plan

Before you begin recruiting, it is important to inventory the talent you have on staff, find a fair way to trim away those who don't fit the profile, and focus your attention on retaining those who do. Conduct "stay interviews" with staff you want to retain, to find out what it will take to make them happy. Remember that some employees desire increased responsibility and challenging work more than salary increases. Stay interviews allow you to find out what motivates your staff and brings out their best performance.

The next step is to start recruiting. Your ability to hire the person you want is always impacted by the hiring environment. You may be looking for an employee with a profile that is in short supply, or you may be able to easily identify numerous candidates for your position. Analyzing the recruiting environment and developing a strategy that will ensure success is the critical component of this step.

What is your competitive edge in the hiring marketplace? Are you hiring an employee that is in high demand? Do you offer top compensation and benefits, work/life balance, and career growth? Often the answer is somewhere in between. Now is the time to honestly assess how your opportunity will be perceived in the current market and to plan your recruiting strategy accordingly.

Bearing in mind the results of the above analysis, the urgency for filling the position, and the internal resources of your firm, you have several options for how you can identify the best possible candidate for your position:

- **Employee Referrals:** This can be a great way of attracting talent to your firm. Many companies offer bonuses to team members for referred candidates who are hired as a result of this process.

- **Advertising:** Effective venues might include local newspapers, trade journals, associations, and job boards.

- **Job Fairs:** When hiring large numbers of team members, a job fair can be an efficient way to quickly assess the market and find good applicants.

- **Contingency Staffing:** Employing the use of a contingency staffing firm will assist you in finding candidates quickly and in identifying a portion of the "passive candidates" in the market. Fees are paid by you and are only incurred should you hire a candidate represented by the firm.

- **Retained Search:** A retained search firm collaborates with you to hire a candidate who has been specifically identified by the firm for your position. This approach is generally used when a very specific combination of skills, personal attributes, and abilities is required in the person you plan to hire.

The top candidates should be interviewed a second time. This step may include the use of assessments that are designed to give additional information about the candidate. Either way, a second interview will give you a more in-depth understanding of the person you are considering and give them the chance to learn more about you.

Obtain detailed references for the top individuals who are under consideration. At this point, it is time to compare all of the information you have gathered to the criteria you established at the beginning of the process and make your decision.

In a perfect world, you are now ready to make an offer. Of course this is not a perfect world, so do not be surprised if you find that you are hesitant to move forward. Often during this process, you will discover things about your firm or the candidate market that may cause you to rethink the position.

This could mean starting the search over with a different set of criteria. Or you may decide to create a different position to bring in a talented individual in a different role. If at any point you think you need to adjust your plan, do it! Taking the time to identify and hire the best possible talent for your firm is critical to creating and sustaining a great firm.

Invest in Development

Developing a collaborative culture requires both engagement and intellectual curiosity. The accounting industry is full of people who somehow believe that once they got their CPA credential that they can stop going to school. Or, they believe that "training and development" begins and ends with fulfilling the CPE requirements necessary to maintain credentials.

The development of a team of people who are curious and hungry to increase their knowledge is imperative. Great people are always learning. Great people are curious. The best thing we can do is hire them and set the expectations of continual knowledge building from the day they walk through the doors of the firm.

It is never too late to start. Developing learning plans for each member of the firm, hiring of learning coordinators, and developing an ongoing program to pass knowledge from one generation to the next with a mentoring program is a one-way ticket to success. Sadly, the economic struggles some firms experienced were often used to eliminate this important function. This is the time to build knowledge in the firm—not destroy it.

The Boot Camp Approach

One firm that's found the "secret sauce" is Clark Nuber P.S., a 150-person Bellevue, Washington, firm that's consistently ranked as one of

Washington's best places to work and enjoys a remarkably high 88 percent retention rate.

Tracy White, SPHR,
senior director of human
resources
Clark Nuber P.S.
www.clarknuber.com
Bellevue, Washington

Tracy L. White, SPHR, senior director of human resources, shares these insights into what it takes to build a dedicated staff: "We want to deliver value to clients, provide challenging and rewarding work for our employees and give back to the community," White says. "So we make sure the people we bring in match our core values, have the right work ethic, and know how to communicate. That way we don't face the generational issues some other firms do."

Associates who come aboard get to experience all kinds of work, from commercial and nonprofit assignments to employee benefit audits. "You get to work in all different kinds of industries, so you can make a better decision about where you want your career to go," she says.

Clark Nuber puts new hires through a two-day boot camp that instills core values and builds team spirit. It doesn't stop there. "We have a core curriculum aligned to an expectations grid with separate audit and tax tracks," White says. "It aligns with the core competencies the

AICPA has established, and extends from the associate level through seniors and principals, with a piece aimed at partners as well."

Core competencies start with personal productivity, professional development, practice development, client relations, engagement, and business management and leadership. For each area there are expectations for associates, and the firm ties annual performance reviews to these areas as well as the learning curriculum. "Depending on what the people need in terms of development, they can take different courses over a three-year cycle," White says.

Courseware the firm offers provides continuous learning in "soft" skills, hands-on computer training, and technical skills. In communications, for example, you'll find a course dealing with difficult people as well as a workshop on networking at social events. If someone really needs something, we will send them outside for training.

Clark Nuber has launched its own Leadership Development Institute, which members of the firm apply for and commit to in order to prepare for advancement. At any given time, twenty to thirty people are in the LDI program, she says.

"We offer opportunities for personal growth to everyone in the firm." For example, there's a one-day "It's OK to Be the Boss" program for seniors and above. A recent graduate of that program was inspired to write an e-book called, *It's OK to Manage Your Boss*. White says that will be offered to admins, associates, and anyone else at CN who has a boss.

Her advice to other firms:

- **Offer leading-edge technology.** White says having the right technology tools available makes a big difference in recruiting and retention. "We are always looking for ways to make people more efficient and productive," she says. "And younger people are excited about having the latest tools available.

- **Provide work/life balance.** "We've never been the kind of firm that expects seventy-hour work weeks," White says. In fact, the firm trains its associates in time management so that work gets done without heavy deadline pressure. "We value hard work, but at the same time we don't want people to miss important events in their children's lives," she says. Flex-time arrangements, job sharing, and remote access to the firm's IT resources offer important flexibility.

- **Have some fun.** The CEO and partners recently put on a "Dancing with the Stars" event, taped for posterity and available on YouTube. "You have to make sure people have fun. It's an important part of the culture here."

- **Make sure you have partner buy-in**. "The owners need to see the strategic value to the firm and its future of investing in training and development beyond the minimum," White says. "It has to become part of the culture."

Consider an On-Boarding Program

Clark Nuber's two-day boot camp is a good way to get new hires that come aboard as a class to form friendships and bond with each other.

But you may want to go further, with a formal on-boarding program, which typically covers the critical first ninety days on the job.

Newly hired staff members have often confided to me that they feel like outsiders. They have trouble getting information and spend months proving themselves to others before being trusted with meaningful work assignments.

Much of the time, new employees are younger than current staff members. In addition, firms are hiring more women and people of diversity than ever before. Thus, in addition to facing barriers just because they are new, many new hires have different outlooks and working styles than seasoned staff. This reality adds to the challenge of fostering an environment that supports and includes the diverse array of people now working in our industry.

On-boarding conveys excitement to each new employee by formalizing his or her role as a team member within the firm. In addition, it helps new employees master new job responsibilities as they utilize readily available resources, including mentors and electronic tools. The goal of new employee on-boarding is for new staff members to integrate fully into the new work environment and become fully productive as quickly and efficiently as possible.

Most programs include four major components:

1. **Vision and Values.** Activities and programs familiarize new staff members with the firm's culture, helping them understand their specific responsibilities in fulfilling the firm's strategic plan.

2. **Team Building.** Activities and programs assimilate new staff members into work teams as quickly and productively as possible,

alleviating ambiguity and setting the tone for strong working relationships.

3. **Mentor Program.** New staff members build relationships and navigate unwritten rules by pairing with experienced peers. This system enhances team building, vision, and goals.

4. **Human Resources Orientation.** New employees acquire the logistical information necessary to perform their jobs. This includes benefits enrollment, tours of facilities, information and training on software, etc.

The responsibility for productivity as well as morale falls largely on the shoulders of management. In order to retain newly hired staff for the long run, firms must support managers in acquiring the skills that foster a healthy working environment.

While most people in management understand administration and logistics, few have had any formal training in actually managing other people. As such, firms have no choice other than to provide learning opportunities to fill this gap. Some specific behaviors that should be addressed when training managers are:

- building an inclusive and effective team

- coaching and counseling

- setting performance objectives

- identifying and addressing interpersonal dynamics

- employing effective communication skills

With the necessary support and training in place before on-boarding, managers will be confident and effective in helping new employees become successful members of the team. In addition, the on-boarding process as a whole will more effectively integrate new staff members into the firm.

Now that we've explored the pieces that can help you recruit and develop collaborative team members, in the next chapter, we'll discuss new technologies that enable teams to effectively collaborate anywhere/anytime, with each other and with your clients.

Visit www.boomer.com/collaboration and download

Collaboration Tool #10

Your Collaborative Employee Engagement Plan

Chapter Eleven: Technology Tools that Simplify Collaboration

It's traditional at Mitchum, Jones & Templeton for the partners to meet after hours on the last Friday of the month for a happy hour. Two fingers of scotch were already poured over ice in three crystal glasses from the minibar in the conference room.

"Here's to another good month," said Tom Mitchum, raising his glass. "And more to come."

"Here, here!" said Sam Jones and Bill Templeton, nearly in unison. Bill added, "It sure looks like we are on the right track."

Sam paused. "I have something to tell you both, and I can't think of a better time."

"What's on your mind, Sam?" said Tom.

"I've been doing a lot of soul searching lately, and I've decided to move on," Sam said with a shrug. "I've tried to get my arms around all the culture changes you've been making...but it's just not working for me. I liked things the way they were and don't want to hold you two back."

"We go back a long way," Bill said. "My wife says we finish each other's sentences, for Pete's sake. I had a feeling this was coming."

Tom nodded his head. "I can't say I'm surprised, either. But it's real important that we make this transition as easy as possible, with no hard feelings. I for one would like to work something out so that we don't lose all the tax knowledge you have in your head. That's meant a lot to the firm and our clients."

Bill rattled the ice in his glass and walked to the bar for a refill. "I think there's a way we can do that. Let's bite the bullet and invest in that knowledge management software we've been talking about. I hear it's a great way to capture what they call intellectual capital."

"Geez…something else I've got to get used to?" Sam moaned. "Can't I just be available over the phone? I'm OK with having some kind of consulting contract going forward. In fact, that is what I was planning to propose. There's a phone at my lake cottage."

"You better take a cell phone with you out on that lake," Tom said and laughed. "You can keep it on vibrate so it won't scare away the bass."

The three laughed together at that. "OK, you win," Sam said. "We can work something out."

"But speaking of transitions," Tom said, "Sally moving to North Carolina gives us an opportunity we should not pass up. I want to set her up with a mirror-image system down there and videoconferencing. She is just too sharp to let go, and there's plenty of business available in the Research Triangle."

"That's a great idea," Bill chimed in. "She could eventually open an office for us down there. I bet she'd jump at a chance like that. If she does well, it could give her a path to partnership."

"With her energy and collaborative work style, it just might work," Tom said. "Especially since she'll maintain access to Sam's tax expertise. Working remotely from home will make it easier for her with a baby on the way, too. We'll find a way to accommodate her—I bet she won't want to be a stay-at-home mom."

Sam shook his head. "Now I know I'm doing the right thing." Then he raised his glass. "Here's to successful transitions."

■

Just like the partners at the fictional Mitchum, Jones & Templeton, technology is having a huge impact on the accounting profession, at firms large and small. And, getting technology "right" is more important than ever. Historically it's been used to make back office procedures more efficient, but it's now being used to deliver greater value to clients—including improved collaboration.

In the 2012 CCH Technology Survey, 64 percent of firms surveyed placed top priority on how technology could enhance client service, with cloud and mobile technologies delivering the ability to:

- work anytime, anywhere

- serve clients in any location

- improve security and backup procedures

- boost collaboration with clients

In addition to improved client service, the top reasons for adopting cloud/mobile devices include increased productivity and improved work/life balance. Cloud computing and the use of smartphones and tablets are tightly intertwined, according to the CCH report.

Mobile devices, of course, are ideal for connecting to cloud-based services when out of the office, a scenario becoming increasingly common in the accounting profession. More than 80 percent of accountants reported doing some work outside the office, most often involving client visits, both local and out of town. Also popular was doing work from a home office.

Across firms of all sizes, accountants prefer iPhones and iPads over smartphones and tablets running other operating systems. Android devices ranked second, with BlackBerry devices a distant third.

Missing Ingredient: A Technology Plan

Eighty-seven percent of the accountants surveyed by CCH said that their firms could be doing more to leverage technology, but fewer than 15 percent said they were very confident in the ability of their firms to understand and manage emerging technologies.

The survey found that most firms do not have a written plan for emerging technologies. Only 4 percent of small firms (fewer than ten employees) have such plans, compared with 35 percent of midsize firms (ten to forty-nine employees) and 46 percent of large firms (fifty or more employees).

Firms are further along in adopting, or preparing to adopt, new technologies. For example, 90 percent of large firms either already have implemented or will add smartphones and expand social media marketing within three years. Also quickly becoming part of the technology foundation for large firms are cloud and software as a service (84 percent) and tablets (74 percent).

Talley & Company: From $5,000 per year to $60,000

One firm that's got technology right is Talley & Company, based in Orange, California. Managing Principal Andrew Talley, CPA, JD, says that technology makes a huge difference when it comes to collaboration. "We are in a changing environment, because of changing client expectations and the expanded services you need to provide," he says.

"People are not looking for a tax professional per se, but a business advisor. That requires a group of individuals, because no one person can know everything. What you need is a team of subject matter experts who collaboratively work together for the good of the client."

Andrew Talley, CPA, JD,
managing principal
Talley & Company
www.talleynco.com
Orange, California

One example: The firm recently turned a $5,000 per year client into a $60,000 one, expanding the relationship to offer back-office transactional functions like bookkeeping and payroll on an outsourced basis. "We were able to save them over three percent on their accounting function spend—over one hundred thousand dollars in their case—and further reduce the business risk associated with things like workers' comp and SDI, plus deliver management metrics they weren't getting because they did not have a CPA on staff."

Collaborative technologies add value in ways that may not be obvious at first blush. "We have been able to access talent across the country because of technology, Talley says. "The firm has a cloud-based system that people can log into from their home and integrate with us as though they are in our office. So that dynamic where you tear down the walls and eliminate geography as a barrier has dramatically increased our ability to serve clients and at a much higher level."

Talley explains: "Our office is in Southern California, an area where skills are in high demand, with Big Four and Tier Two firms all hunting for the same high-level people. But because we are cloud-based, I can obtain the skills I need anywhere in the country, and they can log into our system from home."

For example, Talley found a senior tax person five states away to do review-level work for the firm on a per diem basis. "I have a professor from a junior college who is doing controllership work for us, for pennies on the dollar compared to what we would have to pay to hire someone internally. And on the admin side, I have someone on the East Coast who is doing our A/R and collection work."

Another payoff comes from flexibility. "From a recruiting or staffing standpoint, I can provide something other firms cannot," Talley says. "I have a tax manager who's been with me twenty-two years, who would traditionally have to spend tax season in the office away from her family. Now she picks the kids up from school, makes dinner for them, and later in the evening logs back in to complete her work. She is actually more productive now than ever. In the past two years, she's put in more billable time than in the previous twenty. All because of flexibility."

He sums it up this way: "If you take technology out of the equation, you are back to square one. You have gen X, gen Y, and millenials who are looking for a team approach, not an autonomous, 'island' approach where I am the professional know-it-all. And until the owners create the kind of environment where younger staff can flourish, they are going to have a hard time. The younger generations are production oriented and probably more risk/reward oriented than the current generation of leaders. You cannot just dangle the carrot, because they will move on."

Hartmann, Blackmon & Kilgore PC: Ahead of the Curve

"We are willing to try most anything when it comes to technology, which is different from how most accountants think," says Dennis Sherrin, CPA, managing shareholder at Alabama-based Hartmann, Blackmon & Kilgore PC. Over the years, the Mobile Bay firm grew to fifty employees and seven partners in four offices spread across southeast Alabama.

Dennis Sherrin, CPA,
managing shareholder
Hartmann, Blackmon & Kilgore PC
www.hbkcpas.com
Mobile Bay, Alabama

The firm ended up with a lot of redundancies in the IT area. Each office had its own IT staff and its own network and software, Sherrin says. "We decided to centralize and keep everything in one location, and out of that came a cloud-based workflow management system. Now any professional in any office can pull up client records and work on a return," he says. "It's resulted in at least a ten percent savings in our spend on tax prep—that's tremendous in our business."

Collaboration extends to the audit and accounting side of the practice as well, Sherrin says. "We have many clients on Xero, which is a cloud-based accounting product that is very collaborative. We work with them on real-time information because Xero eliminates after-the-fact data entry using daily bank feeds. Clients can open a dashboard and see graphically where they stand day-to-day, and that is where accounting is going in the future."

Everyone in the firm has remote access via the centralized Citrix network, so they can log in anywhere, anytime, as if they were at a desk in the office. "Our audit staff, for example, can connect to our servers from client sites in California or Texas." That includes a key employee who relocated to Mississippi nine years ago and has worked for the firm remotely ever since. "We didn't want to lose him," Sherrin says.

The move toward collaborative technologies coincided with another strategic decision the shareholders made about four years ago. Sherrin explains it this way: "We decided to move away from the old culture of top-down management and start thinking more like one firm. Out of that we wanted to make sure all our people have skin in the game. So we developed a committee approach, led by our managers. Now we have committees for technology, training and development, tax, and audit. Soon we will add a marketing committee as well. We have a Leadership Academy with twelve people who are our rising stars. They are learning about practice management and understanding how teams work."

A recent success: The technology committee took on the task of finding a better phone system, developing the parameters, and interviewing vendors. "They did all that before they ever came to me with a recommendation," Sherrin says. "The solution they found will work across all our offices, and the transition will be seamless compared to how it once was."

The payoff: "Since we started advocating technology over the past five years, we've had revenue growth of thirty percent—the BP oil spill slowed us down a bit. Overall realization is up seven to twelve percent, but that is tough to pin down because we are going to value pricing for some of what we do."

Tools that Keep Your Team Connected

The right tools will allow team members in any location to connect instantly and capture information that can be organized, stored securely, and shared as needed.

Collaboration tools range from e-mail to videoconferencing to sophisticated knowledge management platforms. E-mail and instant messaging are best for short conversations that don't need to be shared. "If more people need to be involved, use a collaborative workspace tool such as SharePoint or Microsoft 360," says Jim Boomer, CIO and shareholder at Boomer Consulting, Inc. "If knowledge needs to be captured for future reference, use a knowledge management system."

The long-term payoffs of installing a firm-wide knowledge management solution are significant. A knowledge management system will help promote the capturing of knowledge that people keep in their heads and keep your firm from losing vital intellectual capital if key people leave—or are reluctant to share because they want to ensure job security.

As seasoned professionals start to retire, many firms face the risk that a big chunk of knowledge will walk out the door with these retiring professionals. Without a formal knowledge management system in place, much of the tacit knowledge that individuals assume everyone else knows won't be missed until it has already left the firm.

Beyond the leadership and generational shift that the profession faces over the next few years, knowledge sharing and collaboration are simply operational best practices. Firms that share knowledge are more collaborative, efficient, and profitable. Some questions come quickly to mind:

- How often are the same questions asked again and again (in per-son or in e-mail), when the answers could be captured in a system and easily looked up?

- Does the firm have a consistent position from one office to anoth-er on critical business or tax issues? Or do practitioners in different offices provide different answers? How much duplication of effort is involved?

Most high-end knowledge management products include a docu-ment management component or integrate with one. Other features that add efficiency and promote collaboration across the firm include expert profiles, online Q&A capability, collaboration, and project workspace.

"Collaborative technologies will never replace face-to-face conversa-tions," says Boomer. "There are facial expressions you can't replicate in a virtual environment." But multipoint videoconferencing with Skype, OOVOO, or the new Microsoft Office 365 makes it easier and more affordable. Half the staff at Boomer Consulting works remotely, and they connect via Skype and SharePoint. "It's amazing what a step up that is from just having a teleconference."

Boomer shares these keys to getting a high payoff:

- **Examine your processes.** "Start by analyzing how you do things and how work gets shared," Boomer says. "Then apply technology where it fits best, and train people so they are clear on which tool to use for what."

- **Get buy-in from the top down.** "If you don't have critical mass on the platform, it's going to fall short," he says. "Buy-in starts at the top of the firm. Leaders who continue to work outside the system will undercut their own initiative."

- **Showcase your quick wins.** "Show how collaboration has helped the firm, on the revenue side or the cost-saving side," Boomer says. "Show how collaborating brought in new business or eliminated waste. That will get more people on board."

Finding Success with Remote Workers

Remote work is becoming more common, and it's important to find ways your team can collaborate from multiple locations. The Telework Research Network reports that telecommuting grew by 73 percent between 2005 and 2011. In Boomer Consulting's, Inc's 2013 Mobile Device Trends Survey of professionals in the accounting industry, 63 percent of firms said they have remote workers. These statistics confirm the growing importance of technology and the need for effective collaborative tools that make remote work possible.

Like the fictional partners at Mitchum, Jones & Templeton, leaders at many firms differ on remote work; whether you resist it or fully accept the idea, learning more about the real-world issues can help. Here is a look at the opportunities and challenges faced by one remote worker, Arianna Campbell of Boomer Consulting. Two years ago she moved to North Carolina from Boomer's Manhattan, Kansas, office. In her own words:

My work situation may be considered nontraditional by many in the accounting industry, but changes in technology and firm culture are making flexible work arrangements more mainstream. However, as I have experienced firsthand, transitioning to a new way of working is a learning process for everyone involved. Here are a few lessons learned:

Lesson 1: Support for Remote Working Starts at the Top. The leadership of the company sets the example that others will follow. Boomer Consulting, Inc. owners Gary Boomer, Sandra Wiley, and Jim Boomer understand that a workplace is not defined by physical boundaries. They are united in their thinking that *how* you work is more important than *where* you work. This commitment to remote working is communicated to the Boomer Consulting, Inc. staff by investment in technology, continual training, and support of remote team members.

In addition, all three owners are focused on the results of the work instead of micromanaging the process of how the work is completed. Jim Boomer explains this in more detail in his article, "Build a Culture of Accountability in 2013":

"If employees are meeting the goals that were outlined and agreed upon at the beginning of the quarter, it doesn't really matter how many hours they put in or if they checked their Facebook hourly. If employees are truly not working enough hours or if they are seemingly wasting excessive amounts of time, the results will speak for themselves. And results are what you're really after."

This kind of leadership creates a firm culture that removes many of the roadblocks to remote working. With support from the top, and the technology to make it happen, remote working becomes a reality.

Lesson 2: Technology Makes Remote Working Possible. When I moved, the hardware that I had at my desk in the office was packed up and shipped to North Carolina (including laptop, two twenty-four-inch monitors, printer/scanner/fax, webcam, desk phone, headset, etc.). Since I do not have IT support on location, I set everything up myself—and I am not tech savvy at all. This is a testament to the efforts of Director of Technology Eric Benson, who faces the challenge of choosing hardware solutions that are advanced enough to handle our needs but simple enough for remote employees to understand and assemble. Eric has never seen my office, but in the event that he did need to do any visual IT troubleshooting, we would use screen sharing and/or video conferencing so he could see the issue. We continue to find that moving further into the digital workplace drives innovation.

In addition to company-owned hardware, I use my personal devices. My Android phone and tablet both have apps for company e-mail, interoffice instant messenger, and our VOIP phone system. I use my mobile phone for work-related texts and standard phone calls as well. We are in the process of moving to new platforms for our CRM and document storage systems, and both of these have apps that allow me to access information anytime, anywhere.

All firm apps are password protected, and our Exchange server settings require my phone and tablet to be password protected. My devices time out after five seconds, and I cannot change the required password or time out settings. I feel better knowing that the firm data is protected by multiple passwords and other security measures. I have found that the convenience of being able to work from anywhere outweighs any hassle of having to enter my password every time I use my personal devices.

Lesson 3: Communication Can Make or Break Remote Working. Support from leadership and integrated technology solutions are important, but communication is the glue that holds the team together. Communication builds team relationships, strengthens firm culture, keeps processes running smoothly, and allows the team to provide a high level of client service. When you have remote workers, it takes a proactive approach to keep the lines of communication open.

There are several ways team members communicate here at Boomer Consulting, Inc.:

- Staying in touch on a daily basis is a challenge, so it is important to find ways to "stop by" and say hello. We use our interoffice instant messenger system as a quick way to say hello. This our virtual way of dropping by someone's desk to say good morning or to ask a quick question.

- For a consistent and intentional connection, we have a weekly staff meeting when everyone on the team (including the owners) calls in and shares updates and announcements.

- I have weekly one-on-one calls with each of my supervisors (Jim Boomer and Sandra Wiley) via Skype. This face-to-face interaction is an important part of our communication. It helps us connect on a personal level in a way that is not possible by just talking on the phone. Being able to read expressions and body language leads to clearer communication and lessens chances for misinterpretations.

- We also use video conferencing for our quarterly company strategic plan update meetings. Every ninety days we take time to make sure that we are staying on track with our strategic plan for the year. Everyone on the team participates, and I join via videoconference.

- While technology can bring us close together as a team, nothing replaces in-person meetings. I travel three times a year to meet with the team, and we arrange this around specific team events, maximizing the use of the time together.

Lesson 4: Work/Life Boundary Decisions Must Be Made. When I tell people I work remotely, they say, "Oh, that must be nice!" and stare off into space as they dream up pictures of lounging on the couch, eating junk food, and watching daytime television while a computer sits neglected in a distant corner. This is not the reality. Working remotely does not change your workload; it forces you to define your boundaries. Being able to log on anytime from anywhere challenges you to draw a line between work and life, between home and office, between a cell phone and a CRM system, between an afternoon with your children and one last e-mail that you have to send to a client.

In my opinion, you need to define where work ends and where your personal life begins, and this is different than work/life balance. Every person who is employed has to make this decision to some degree, but as a remote worker, I have found the gray area is almost infinite until you set your boundaries. This is a personal decision, but it is one that must be made. Doing so will increase focus, improve efficiency, and increase the quality of both work and life for everyone involved.

In the next chapter we'll talk about our predictions for the future of the profession, what firms can to do get ready, and strategic planning steps to take now.

■

Visit www.boomer.com/collaboration and download

Collaboration Tool #11

Building Your Technology Plan

Chapter Twelve: Where Do We Go From Here?

As I look ahead to the future of our profession, I see more firms following the path we've watched Mitchum, Jones & Templeton take through each chapter in this book. Faced with losing key accounts to another firm and the loss of talented staff, partners Tom Mitchum, Sam Jones, and Bill Templeton chose to change the firm's culture, from the inside out, following a shared vision.

Take a "Best Resources" Approach for More Leverage

While MJ&T is clearly fictional, real-life firms of all sizes face the same kinds of challenges. I believe that successful firms need to move away from the traditional silos that still affect so many firms today. It starts at the top, with owners who think in terms of "his book of business, her book of business, and my book of business" making a true commitment to change. That silo thinking extends to the way firms are organized, and people get pigeonholed because "that person works for him, and this person works with me." The result is that work gets distributed in a linear way, from the top down, throughout the firm.

Adopting "best practices" has become commonplace, and I believe a logical extension of that concept is a "best resources" approach. The idea is to pull together the best resources, based on the talent you have available in the firm, in order to serve the client needs most effectively and deliver the highest possible value. The thought process needs to be more like "I need help with this client, and the best person to help me is so-and-so because she has the skills and knowledge." It could be another partner, a subject matter expert, a person with the right computer skills, or someone who is better at writing or presenting.

Moving toward that kind of collaborative environment is not an easy thing, but it is essential for long-term success. It will upset the apple cart inside many firms, in almost every area, ranging from the compensation model to how firms manage performance and train people—especially future leaders, who will need soft skills more than ever.

No More Lone Rangers: Encourage Group Thinking

Today, when a new idea develops in a firm, it is often one leader coming to the group and selling his or her idea. Then, the idea is implemented by a committee. In the future, the idea will be developed by a group of people from the inception, and then the entire group will continue to support and nurture the idea by bringing in other team members as needed to make the idea better. The thought process is "let's all sit down at the table and figure this out—together."

A pattern will develop, which ultimately make a good idea a great idea: by pulling together everyone's ideas, thoughts, intellectual capital, the firm will benefit from the "group think" rather than "individual think." As you might imagine, there will be little room for individual egos in this environment. Silos within the firm will deteriorate, and power teams will emerge.

Embrace Diversity

Firms today have a reputation for being predominantly male, white, and aging at the partner level; female, middle-aged, and white at the manager level; and slightly more diverse in race, gender, and nationality at the staff level. Given the changing demographics of our country today, and the reality that our younger leaders have a more diverse and global outlook of the world, it is safe to say that the look of our firms will change in the future. We are going to have to be more colorful and more widespread in our human resources.

This is a welcome change by our younger leaders who have gone to school and often traveled the world with friends of different nationalities and cultures. Additionally, this change will require that we put a stronger emphasis on retention, attraction, and motivation of the best talent and find new ways to solidify our teams.

Consider New Ways to Keep Score

In the past, the most valuable people have been the partners, or the rainmakers. But in a collaborative model, you see value coming from every single person in the firm. They all bring different skills to the table, they all contribute, and that makes everyone more valuable.

The way most firms are organized today follows the classic pyramid shape, narrow at the top and broad at the base. The pyramid is inverted when it comes to compensation, so most of the rewards stay at the top. But as collaboration takes hold, firms will flatten out a bit more, and wealth will need to be distributed differently, because firms need to attract, reward, and retrain talent throughout the firm to deliver the value clients expect.

A closely related issue is hourly billing, a traditional way firms "keep score." We see the hourly model falling by the wayside, in favor of value pricing and negotiated annual contracts, covering a range of services. When projects or engagements are priced properly, value will far exceed the amount of time actually involved in getting the work out—especially as technology further streamlines labor-intensive processes.

We introduced you to Andy Talley in the last chapter. He puts it this way: "The traditional, top-down, I-am-the-expert approach is very much going away. What we have is a group of subject matter experts who collaboratively work together for the good of the client. That's required now because of the expanded services you need to provide. It's uncomfortable because there is a certain level of loss of control in that." I certainly agree. At Boomer Consulting, Inc. we are firm believers in all of this, but there are times when I have to check myself, because I tend to think, "Maybe an owner should be doing that, or a higher level person, or someone who has been here longer." That is just not true anymore, and thinking that way will hold firms back.

Replace the Ladder with a Lattice

In the classic pyramid structure, you moved up the pyramid over a period of years, and if you were not "partner material," at a certain point you got outplaced to a client. Today, there are a lot of younger people who have different career goals in mind. They may not want to be on the so-called "partner track" but want to develop subject expertise and get rewarded for that without having to deal with everything partners must.

Some people feel that you need to follow specific steps up the ladder to get to partnership, and if you do not do that, you are less valuable to the firm. That happened to women for years, and now it applies to men as well. Somewhere along that path, if you decide to move sideways or off the board for a while, have children and come back later, you are seen as an outlier, someone who doesn't bring as much value to the firm.

Moving forward, successful firms will need to replace that career ladder with a lattice or matrix structure. In that setting, you can move up or sideways, back a little, or up and to the right—and people will still see your value.

Set Up a Future Leader Initiative

Putting together a collaborative leadership team geared for the future requires looking at each person as a separate and unique individual—identifying the unique characteristics that they have and allowing them to develop those skills. Just because someone is not the best business developer does not mean they are not valuable; they may indeed have a gift for putting processes in place that will save the firm hours in productivity and efficiency. Another person who is a superb business developer may not like to research new systems. His or her motivation may come from front-end projects, dealing with clients and prospects. One is not wrong or less valuable; both are equally amazing. A positive way to find out what is floating around in your future leaders' minds is to form a "Tomorrows Leaders Initiative" in your firm. Give them objectives, but let them figure out the strategies, ideas, and timelines for initiatives that will help your firm prepare for the changes ahead.

Prepare for the Journey Ahead

If you've read this far in the book and seen how other firms are benefiting from collaboration, it's a safe bet you've "bought in" to the idea and want to make changes in your firm, too. However, you may be wondering where to begin.

As a first step, the owners have to ask, "Are we doing this just for ourselves and just want to close the doors when we leave, or are we doing this to create a firm that lives on after we are gone?" If you want the firm to continue after you are gone, you have to take some risks and start thinking differently and more deeply.

On the other hand, if you say, "It's all about me," then just keep doing what you are doing until you can't. Forget the collaborative model, and just sail the ship until it falls off the end of the earth.

This book should be used as a roadmap and a guide for making collaboration a reality in your firm. Put together a task force and start at the beginning of the book and work through the exercises at the end of each chapter. There will be hard work involved, but the tools and resources provided will help the firm figure out the changes that need to be made going forward.

Determine a Timeline for Change

You cannot wait ten years to decide whether or not to do this. Now is the time, because changing a firm's culture takes time. You have to start turning the wheel now. If you don't, you will be so far behind the curve that when you decide to make changes, it will be too late and you will get left behind.

As a strong word of advice, the amount of time involved to make significant changes in culture depends on three things: the leadership you have in place, the talent you have available in the firm, and the commitment among the partners. Three years is a reasonable timeframe, and five is probably too long.

If you have a partner group that is committed, you can see major culture changes in a year or two. But if you have *one partner* who is behind the curve and isn't really excited about it or doesn't really believe in it, that can hold you back. If someone tells me it took them five years to change their culture, I say to them, "You had someone who was really getting in the way."

Consider a Firm Summit

I like the term "summit" because "retreat" implies you are looking at the past and moving backward. "Summit" feels both more ambitious and at the same time implies a broader participation base. The idea is to bring the firm's leaders and members together along with outside expertise and facilitation to initiate strategies for exponential growth.

As we said earlier, most firms spend too little time working *on* the firm and too much time working *in* the firm, especially in firms where governance is not well defined. If everyone believes he or she is in charge but too busy to lead, then little growth takes place. Here are some tips for holding a summit on culture change:

- **Select a venue away from the office.** Get people out of their daily routine. Meetings at the office just do not work as well, because of too many interruptions. You want people thinking strategic thoughts and sharing ideas, not fielding client calls.

- **Be inclusive, not exclusive.** Fresh ideas and "new blood" should be welcome. Include managers and staff, especially since the subject is building a collaborative culture.

- **Use a professional facilitator.** An experienced facilitator keeps participants focused and on the agenda. It is difficult, if not impossible, to facilitate your own firm summit. You might be surprised at how focused participants become when an outsider is involved. Using a professional facilitator also ensures the firm summit will happen as scheduled.

- **Start on a positive note.** Take time to celebrate and be grateful for your successes. This exercise requires mere minutes but is often overlooked. Take a little time to reflect on the most positive events during the past year, why they were important, and if any follow-up is needed. Better decisions result when participants feel confident and positive.

- **Work from an agenda, and stay on time.** Don't surprise participants. Solicit agenda items in advance, and distribute an agenda with meeting materials. Do your homework prior to the meeting. Keep each item strategic, and stay on time.

- **Stick to concepts.** Force participants to think in terms of the big picture. The tendency is to focus on tactical rather than strategic issues. Tell participants up front to avoid restraints such as budget and time. It pays to dream. You will find the time and budget for great ideas and strategies. The chances of identifying great ideas and strategies are diminished greatly if you start with the premise, "We can't afford that." Think in terms of who can "pull this off" or "whom do we know that can help us?"

- **Set up task forces for follow-up.** Each person must be held accountable for his or her part. Allow those responsible an opportunity to agree upon due dates, which will ensure the chance of each project being completed on time. This is all part of leveraging your firm's resources.

Look Outside Your Organization

In a recent article on collaborative leadership, my colleague Jim Boomer made a good point: The best firms in our profession realize the wealth of information and experience that exists beyond the barriers of their own organization. They typically join one or more peer communities to gain outside ideas and fresh perspectives. They also recognize the importance of peer accountability in that it's a lot easier to tell yourself and your team you didn't accomplish something than it is to tell your peer.

If you're still trying to go at it alone, I would encourage you to look into joining a peer community. We started The Boomer Technology Circles™ over a decade ago and now have a number of other specialized communities of leading firms pushing each other to get better:

- The Boomer Technology Circles™ community will help your firm bridge the gap between technology and practice management and accelerate your progress through thought leadership and peer accountability.

- The CIO Advantage™ community prepares technology professionals for a seat at the management table by developing their business and IT acumen.

- The CEO Advantage™ is a community of managing partners who act as a collaborative think tank to challenge, encourage, and propel each other to a higher level of success.

- The Talent Development Advantage™ is a community of HR, learning, and human capital leaders focused on talent development through shared intellectual capital, peer networking, and collaboration.

- The Producer Circle™ is a community of business- and IT-savvy thought leaders focused on providing improved client accounting service and achieving firm growth and profitability by leveraging technology and the cloud.

As your firm participates in peer communities and attends training or conferences, it's important to maintain a collaborative mind-set. You'll often get a bigger return on your investment by having cross-functional attendance at these events. This allows for real-time reconciliation of diverse perspectives based on the same information. You don't get this when each party attends their own event and then tries to resolve their differences back at the office. What you usually end up with is little to no buy-in and no execution.

Beyond cross-functional involvement, leadership involvement is also critical. Bringing back a bunch of great ideas from outside the organization is great, but if leadership doesn't buy in, it doesn't go anywhere. Seeing is believing. When firm leaders attend alongside the functional leaders, they will see, believe, and make sure stuff happens.

The pace of change is increasing in our profession, in our country, and in our world. No one can be expected to keep up with the changing environment of practice, technology, HR, tax, and other issues. True leaders recognize this fact and recruit a network of talented individuals both inside and outside their firm so they have the best information possible to make the best business decisions to improve their firm's performance, profitability, and growth. They are truly collaborative leaders.

As a leader in your firm, commit, practice, and engage in the process!

Visit www.boomer.com/collaboration and download

Collaboration Tool #12

Pulling It All Together—Your Collaboration Action Plan

About the Author

Sandra Wiley is a shareholder and the chief operating officer at Boomer Consulting. She is ranked by *Accounting Today* as one of the one hundred most influential people in accounting and as one of the twenty most powerful women in accounting by CPA Practice Advisor. She is an expert in the area of talent development with a passion for leadership development, training, and strategic collaboration. Sandra is a certified Kolbe™ trainer who advises firms on building balanced teams, managing employee conflict, and hiring staff. Sandra is a naturally gifted public speaker who is noted for the energy and excitement she brings to an audience. At the same time, she adds a personal touch that leaves individuals in the crowd with a sense that she is their friend. This ability to build relationships and project warmth makes Sandra especially effective at building great teams. She is a team player in her own right, offering her multitasking skills and a realistic viewpoint that can keep an agenda on track and people focused on the tasks at hand. She is a popular author who is frequently published by many trade journals, including *CPA Practice Management Report*, *Accounting Today*, *Accounting Web*, *The CPA Practice Management Forum*, *The CPA Report of South Carolina*, *Lagniappe* (Society of Louisiana CPAs), and *The Asset* (Missouri Society of CPAs).

Made in the USA
Charleston, SC
17 August 2014